POPULISM AND ECONOMICS

ALSO BY CHARLES DUMAS AND PUBLISHED BY PROFILE

The American Phoenix: And Why China and Europe Will Struggle After the Coming Slump (2011)

Globalisation Fractures: How Major Nations' Interests are Now in Conflict (2010)

China and America: A Time of Reckoning (2008)

The Bill from the China Shop: How Asia's Savings Glut Threatens the World Economy (2006)

POPULISM AND ECONOMICS

Charles Dumas

P

PROFILE BOOKS

First published in Great Britain in 2018 by
Profile Books Ltd
3 Holford Yard
Bevin Way
London WC1X 9HD
www.profilebooks.com

Typeset in Garamond by MacGuru Ltd

Printed and bound in Great Britain by
Clays Ltd, Elcograf S.p.A.

A CIP catalogue record for this book is available from the British Library.

ISBN 978 1 78816 189 3

FSC www.fsc.org
MIX
Paper from responsible sources
FSC® C018072

Contents

List of figures

Introduction: neo-Luddite discontents

Here we are, a quarter-century after the 'end of history', contemplating a possible end to the new world order, while large swathes of middle-income jobs are being taken over by robots.

The decisive discrediting and collapse of communism in 1989–91, with the dissolution of the Soviet Union, appeared to sanctify the world economic order based on democracy and free markets. It left the United States as the sole effective superpower. A blend of capitalism and democracy seemed the ideal political and social system, ending 'history'. Yet the resulting globalisation, with increasingly free worldwide trade and capital movements, and rising migration flows, was followed within seventeen years by the worst financial and economic crisis since the 1930s Great Depression (that in turn had spawned World War II). And that crisis is now followed by the apparent disavowal by the United States itself of the system in which it has been paramount.

Equally paramount have been US firms and interests in generating the hi-tech revolution that has during that same quarter-century transformed the way we all live, with great benefit to aggregate human welfare and potential. But hi-tech effects on jobs, lifestyles and the distribution of wealth and income have been an important source of US discontents – arguably more important than globalisation. As China develops its own tech sector, the role of hi-tech in undermining traditional jobs in advanced countries will increasingly predominate over low-wage emerging-market competition. Nonetheless, hi-tech being home-grown for Americans, their politicians prefer blaming the rise of China, rather than hi-tech. Yet we are nowhere near the end of the story when it comes to jobs rendered obsolete by automation and robots.

What these discontents and problems should remind us of is not often raised in economic texts and analysis. Supposedly it was Winston Churchill (always a risky man to quote) who said: 'democracy is the worst system of government – except all the others'. To this truth might be added: capitalism is the worst system of economics – except the alternatives. Crucially, both democracy and capitalism, as systems, come under the heading of 'least bad', rather than 'best' (or even particularly good). Seeking heaven on earth generally creates hell, as centuries of experience of religious and more recently communist rule have reminded us.

This book is chiefly about the problems that have arisen for the democratic parts of the world as a result of the peculiarities of global capitalism. To a modest degree it is also about what we should do about it.

Hi-tech and globalisation have reinforced one another. How could huge swathes of hi-tech jobs have been established in Bangalore, India (rather than the US), were not that same hi-tech available to transmit the services around the world? How could international supply chains be tuned up to the refined, 'just-in-time' discipline of modern production flows and supply chains without hi-tech?

This confluence of massive change has been completed by the global savings glut – more accurately, the Eurasian structural excess of saving in Germany, the countries surrounding it to the north, west and south, plus China, Japan and the Asian Tigers. This vast section of the world economy can only sustain its saving addiction if other countries or sectors run deficits and/or raise their debt levels. Both the financial crisis itself – and its successor, the euro crisis – as well as the sluggish subsequent global recovery, were clear results of these deficits and debts. In the (non-)recovery, deficit-country belt-tightening reinforced the shortage of demand that is the very nature of a savings glut.

This book will describe how this turn of events arose, explaining and putting in context the discontents expressed by the Brexit vote and subsequent British general election, and the November 2016 election of President Trump. It continues from the series of books I wrote before, during and after the crisis, broadly relating it to global financial imbalances. But here we go beyond those earlier analyses by interrelating the effects of globalisation and its imbalances with the forces of technology – in both its beneficial and its threatening aspects – and demographic shifts.

Only by understanding the interplay between the four key elements – globalisation, technology, demography and imbalances – can recent events be fully analysed, and future consequences, along with desirable policy changes, be described. This book continues a series that started with the 2006 publication of *The Bill from the China Shop*, which detailed the meaning of the savings glut and forecast how the global imbalances it gave rise to would cause a US household debt crisis. That book dealt mostly with this fundamental cause of the crisis, rather than covering the financial shenanigans that were its contingent trigger.

The concept of a savings glut was aptly named in March 2005 by the US Federal Reserve's Vice Chairman, Ben Bernanke. I had introduced the idea earlier, in September 2004, referring to 'Eurasian saving excesses' rather than Mr Bernanke's 'global' glut. (It never has been global.) Aside from the name, my major difference with Bernanke was my forecast that continued excessive Eurasian saving could *cause* a US household debt crisis, as indeed happened in 2007–8. What is especially regrettable about Bernanke's failure to drive through to that conclusion in 2005–7 was that he could then have handled the crisis much better, from his vantage point as Chairman of the Fed (from 2006 – and before that Vice Chairman).

After an interim, mid-crisis look at the same issues in *China and America* (May 2008, pre-'Lehman'), my 2010 *Globalisation Fractures* was a definitive analysis of both the origins and the effects of the imbalances. In 2011, *The American Phoenix* exposed the fallacy of widespread distortions arising from premature faith in China's coming economic supremacy.

Do we now have to contemplate a possible retreat from globalisation itself, rather than merely dealing with its flaws? The neo-Luddites amongst those that voted for Brexit and Trump have been joined by a wave of populist voters in continental Europe. It is vital that the label 'populism' does not become a sneer. To be sure, demagogues have readily exploited widespread discontent with quack remedies. But centrist politicians and commentators have shown equally widespread lack of empathy with the legitimate grievances that underlie this neo-Luddism. The way combined globalisation, technology, demographics and financial imbalances are developing could only too easily aggravate neo-Luddism in future, as well as false ethnic and/or regional divisions.

The savings glut has continued to be a major cause of trouble. In Chapter 2 below, the meaning of 'savings glut' will be fully explained, as well as its strange form in today's world. In no way is this savings glut a necessary (or natural) accompaniment of globalisation, nor is it even indirectly caused by hi-tech breakthroughs. But remarkably, the excess of saving well beyond the scope for needed or profitable investment in the world economy has not just played a major role in provoking the crisis itself (as detailed in my earlier books). It has contributed mightily to

- the poor recovery since the crisis, especially in 2011–16
- key aspects of the increased inequality of income that has accompanied and contributed to the weakness of recovery
- the apparently sharp supply-side drop in potential growth, as well as slower actual growth of Western economies

- the threat that current global financial imbalances may lead to a further economic downswing in late 2019 and 2020, reinforcing disenchantment with globalisation in a crucial US election year.

Combined post-crisis demand constraint, increased inequality, loss of jobs and professional pride as technology renders obsolete many traditional functions has already imposed huge strains. With slower potential growth in future years, this could continue to fuel the dangerous wave of political discontent threatening the world economic order.

One peculiarity is that discontent has been most vigorously expressed in the 'Anglo-Saxon' countries, the US and UK – yet these two countries' people have had larger gains of real after-tax incomes this century than have the Japanese or continental Europeans. That these two countries have run the deficits and debt escalation that offsets globally the savings glut points to the latter's central role in causing present discontents.

This book thoroughly analyses Japan's economy, and its social and political ramifications. Likewise, it examines the euro area (EA), whose institutional flaws led to crisis in 2010–13 and drove out discussion of weak real income growth (even in the relatively successful economies like Germany). Political commitment to the euro has meant that shoring up the EA has had priority in EU councils over objective analysis of poor economic performance. The continental elections of 2017 have revealed deep discontent there too, without quite the disruption (yet) of Brexit and Trump. As for the United States, it is the one with the greatest increase of inequality in recent decades, and the largest disruption so far of traditional work patterns by hi-tech, suggesting diversity in the sources of neo-Luddite discontent.

The interaction of hi-tech and globalisation is complicated further by demography. For twenty-five years from 1990 the primary demographic point was that the rapidly developing and/or transforming 'second world' effectively entered the world economy.

This included the Soviet Union and eastern Europe, China (as it swung into a positive reaction to the near-fatal Tiananmen trauma) and India (which was abandoning the 'Harrovian socialism' of the Nehru dynasty dominated by unsuccessful academic development theories). This added 3 billion people to the 1 billion of the first world, with south-east Asia, the 'Asian Tigers', also enthusiastic participants. This massive surge in the supply of labour vis-à-vis capital, together with the peculiarity of the Eurasian savings glut, dominated the unstable economics of 1989–2009.

In the 'third world', with the Middle East undergoing its own traumas, Latin America remained a world on its own – with only the Mexican–US border to create first-world proximity – and Africa remained far from centre-stage, if not off-stage. But since 2015 Middle Easterners and Africans have engaged in major attempted migration to next-door Europe. While Europe's reaction to this has not been quite as negative as Trump's views on the Mexican border, the pressure of this very different group of left-behinds combines with Europe's potential population decline to create potentially both major economic upside and serious social strain.

This story therefore concerns the interaction of four great forces – globalisation, demography, hi-tech and the savings glut – in generating first of all financial instability, but more importantly demand-side weakness, supply-side distortions and peculiarities, slower underlying growth in the West and greater inequality of income in all countries, though not in the world considered as a whole. The faster growth of poorer than wealthier countries has meant that *globally* the distribution of income has become more equal. Yet within virtually every major country, both rich and poor, it has become more unequal.

First therefore, this book will cover the parallel development of globalisation from the 'fall of the Wall' (1989) to 2016, and the emergence of rampant hi-tech with its disruption of traditional industries. We will then see how global imbalances gave rise to the financial crisis of 2007–8, with the resulting Great Recession of 2008–9. Next, the continued distortion of global demand patterns by excessive saving is shown both to have hobbled the world's recovery from that recession, and distorted it towards seriously excessive dependence on dynamic but grotesquely unbalanced China. This demand-orientated analysis explains the bulk of what has happened in 2010–16, including the euro crisis, as well as what did not happen that should have.

But the parallel slide in the growth rate of productive potential is also partly caused by the savings glut. Record-high rates of global saving are mirrored by identical rates of investment. (At the global level investment equals saving by definition.) Normally, more investment means faster growth. Yet the growth of the real net capital stock in the US and Europe has slowed radically. While this partly *reflects* the sluggish recovery (itself a function of the savings glut), it also *helps to slow* potential growth, as capital input is a major supply-side factor generating potential growth. (As with much of this introduction, this summary statement is more fully argued in later chapters.)

How do we explain the paradox of inadequate US and European investment alongside recent record global ratios of capital spending (capex) to output (GDP)? The answer lies partly in the 'crowding-out' of Western investment by China's exorbitant and wasteful capital spending, averaging an inordinate 46–7% of China's GDP in the eight years 2009–16. This has undermined existing industrial capacities worldwide and has slashed the return on capital globally. The crisis and weak recovery had anyhow created a Keynesian liquidity trap, where the rate of interest that would induce recovery was well below zero. China's downward pressure on the return to potential new investment operated in parallel with and contributed to the collapse of interest rates, both nominal and real. So advanced-country capex, already depressed by the 'liquidity trap', had its potential profitability further eroded.

Excessive Chinese capex partly reflects the over-investment and relatively low return on capital typical of Pacific Rim countries for much of the post-World War II period. But it also arose as China in the financial crisis responded to the collapse of its export-led growth model not by reducing its absurd national savings rate of 50% of output, but by stepping up even further its domestic capex extravagance.

Slower potential growth results from a number of causes – the savings glut is one amongst many. Slower growth and slower productivity gains are functions of globalisation – as massive expansion of the world supply of cheap labour naturally tends to expand low-income, low-value jobs – of different countries' population shifts, and of other country-specific behaviour patterns or policies.

In all probability, the measurement of the benefits of hi-tech to the real economy, and particularly consumer welfare, is in any case understated. This reduces the significance of the growth slowdown, but increases the importance of rising inequality. Widespread fears of, or excitement about, such phenomena as self-driving cars, and the huge changes in production and consumption patterns arising from the internet and other hi-tech developments, are not only deployed as explanations of output and productivity trends. They also are credited with undermining conventional output measures – with more and more convincing evidence that the true value of economies is increasingly understated. Hi-tech frequently increases inequality in the very process of advancing the economy.

These thoughts are prime reasons for comparing the current hi-tech breakthroughs with the original Industrial Revolution (1780–1830, say), in which the lift-off from millennia of broadly unchanged average mass incomes started with a gigantic accumulation of capital by the rich, while the condition of the bulk of the population arguably worsened for fifty years – hence the original Luddites.

Increasing inequality of income distribution has worsened economic performance in some respects, as well as aggravating social tensions for much of the past twenty years. A worldwide tendency has been the build-up of business savings rates – depreciation reserves and retained profits. This has been a major inhibition of demand. It has not necessarily raised inequality of wealth or income between *people*, as the immediate alternative to such retention of profit is its distribution as dividends, and the value of the shares held tends to be unaffected by such distribution decisions. Meanwhile, higher retained profits mean a lower rate of distribution, which *reduces* inequality of incomes in the short run.

As explained below, however, whereas excessive retention of profit appears to be simply a cultural norm in Pacific Rim economies (China, Japan and Korea), amongst US and European companies it is closely associated with tax avoidance, which clearly has contributed to greater personal inequality.

Corporate income retention thus breaks down into two separate phenomena. The more important is huge, bottled-up saving of corporate business in Japan, Korea and increasingly China, where capital market disciplines are weak or non-existent for correcting poor business management and the hoarding of unneeded cash. But alongside this, corporate tax structures in many Western countries have led to hoarding of cash in tax havens, when the economy would be better served by its distribution, either as dividends, after payment of tax due, or as repurchase of stock. Analysis of inequality, therefore, has not only to examine the effects of interpersonal inequality, but also the division of income between companies and households, both considered collectively.

After this three-part survey of the global issues – demand-side, supply-side and distributional – the particular contribution to current discontents of individual countries will bring the analysis into focus in relation to the historic, social and political forces at work. This starts with Japan, 'first mover' in the economics of decline, and then China. The last of the savings 'gluttons' is continental Europe, which has slipped into the role almost by accident, through the malignant effects of European monetary union foolishly yoking together highly disparate countries.

The international policy context has been over-emphasis on monetary solutions to economic problems. So-called 'Keynesian' policies were discredited by the great inflation of the 1970s. Beneficial structural, supply-side reforms meet political resistance, as they tend to be painful for key interest groups. The result has been undue dependence on central banks, and this has been damaging in a number of ways. It has contributed to the increasing disaffection of middle-income, 'working-class' voters that was a big source of 2016's UK Brexit vote and the election of President Trump in America.

In principle, demand stimulus by purely monetary means operates to a great extent through boosting wealth, almost inevitably raising inequality – of wealth at least, and subsequently income. By contrast, fiscal stimulus would add political and distributional factors to the policy decisions. Also, over-reliance on monetary rather than fiscal stimulus has been inherently less effective in spurring economic recovery in a deflationary global context.

One immediate problem facing the world is that the search for a rules-based monetary policy – inflation targets for the most part – has become perverse or even self-defeating (as happens in time to most fixed rules). Partly through the weakness of the past ten years' growth, and partly through the supply-side deflationary impact of hi-tech, the natural rate of inflation would appear to be roughly nil in the United States, continental Europe and Japan (see Chapter 9).

Yet central banks are persevering in trying to raise it to 2%. In the process they are boosting asset prices further – further aggravating the inequality of wealth. And if successful, they could provoke a surge of inflation that may well blow through the 2% targets and be followed by a relapse into recession that will be squarely the responsibility of the central banks. What authorities will we respect then?

Lastly, the analysis in this book will attempt to describe what needs to be done to solve the problems described here, as well as what realistically might be done in the likely economic context of the next couple of years. Economic growth since 2009, though weak, has created one of the longest up-cycles on record. How will it end, and how will we cope with it ending?

*

The original Luddites (1780s to roughly 1810), though energetically supported in their day by Lord Byron, have had a bad rap from economists (as well as the then establishment, anyhow no lover of the great poet). As a general historical matter, giving free rein to technical gains and international trade has vastly improved the living conditions of *everybody* over the long term, including the poorest. But both at the time of the original Industrial Revolution and to some degree in our present era of globalisation and hi-tech transformation, large groups of people – the 'left-behinds' – had or have their lives blighted or even ruined by these forces of general progress.

Is/was Luddite behaviour – originally, smashing the machines – a justifiable reaction to this?

Economics is not such a narrow, technical subject as is sometimes said, and neither is it a province of purely utilitarian materialism. Welfare economics is not a branch of left-wing political thought, but simply an attempt to achieve the best *entire* consequences of an action, or policy, or situation. This requires more than some utilitarian ideal of the greatest aggregate benefit for the greatest number of people. Optimal welfare at least requires that changes to the disadvantage of some people, but with overall benefit to the population as a whole, should be accompanied by some compensation for the losers – though probably not full compensation. And if the pace of disruptive economic and/or social change is excessive, this can arguably be a bad thing, even if the changes are ultimately desirable. Judging what is excessive is, of course, the key.

The original Luddites lived in an era when there was no

compensation for the losers. Their skills were rendered obsolete by newly developed machines that were typically operated by fewer, less skilled workers (sound familiar?). When Lord Liverpool was Britain's prime minister (1812–27), in the difficult period after the Napoleonic Wars, fears of insurrection along the lines of the French Revolution led to repressive social policies that even the far from politically ardent Jane Austen drew attention to. *Habeas corpus* was temporarily suspended in 1817.

The British army had before that crushed the Luddites. But with difficulty. The number of soldiers fighting them at one time exceeded those fighting Napoleon's armies in the Peninsular War (1807–14) – the phase of the Napoleonic Wars that secured the emergence of Wellesley, later Duke of Wellington, as Britain's leading soldier. This is a fair indication of the strength of feeling that uncompensated loss of livelihood can induce.

A major difference between 1780–1830 and today's discontents – aside from the much nastier ordinary condition of so many people's lives back then – is today's universal suffrage. The concentration of wealth during the eighteenth century had seriously shrunk the size of the electorate – votes being obtained by dint of property qualifications. Britain's Great Reform Act of 1832 mostly just eased the property qualification; it fell far short of introducing universal suffrage, even for men. Indeed so shrunken was the electorate by land enclosures during the eighteenth century that even after the 1832 reform the electorate was only raised from 500,000 to 800,000, and from a little over 3% of the population to about 5%.

By contrast, the two original modern democracies, the United Kingdom and the United States, have recently engaged through the ballot box in what appears to have been (amongst other things) a collective neo-Luddite revolt against recent radical transformations of Western market economies. These transformations also, as it happens, have involved a major concentration of wealth, if not quite as extreme as in the eighteenth century and the early nineteenth.

1

Globalisation, technology and demographics

Three transformations around 1990 initiated the recent wave of globalisation:

- the 'fall of the Wall' in 1989, liberating central-eastern Europe from communism
- the collapse of the Soviet Union in 1991, not only bringing its constituents into the global market economy but also reinforcing the shift of India away from a semi-Stalinist economic model
- the 'southern tour' of Deng Xiaoping in 1992, turning China back outwards to the world economy after its threatened withdrawal following the trauma of 1989's Tiananmen Square crackdown.

Prior to this series of transformations, the populations of the 'developed world' (North America, Western Europe, Japan and Australasia) totalled 1 billion or so. Latin American countries had stalled in their catch-up efforts, with massive debt crises and hyperinflation in the 1980s. The catch-up achieved by Japan (about to relapse from 1990, as it happens) was mimicked by Korea, Hong Kong and Singapore, with other Asian Tigers also making real progress. But 1990's addition of the old Soviet Comecon bloc, China and India was an aggregate of 3 billion extra people aiming to participate in the world market economy. The potential labour force of the global market economy was tripled or quadrupled. Moreover, the temptation of other countries, e.g. much of Latin America, to pursue dirigiste economic strategies was undermined.

My *Globalisation Fractures* outlined this labour force 'shock' to the world economy in terms of the huge increase in the supply of labour, in a world of highly mobile capital and relatively free trade in goods (outside of agriculture). In a major recent article for Morgan Stanley, Charles Goodhart developed the themes in greater detail. But the impact of these changes has emerged alongside the development of hi-tech, whose lifespan has been similar, with the public commercial use of the internet starting in mid-1989, and growing explosively thereafter. The internet and hi-tech generally, though dominated by its US originators, is inherently global, with electronic communication not easily contained within national boundaries. These two revolutions in the world economy therefore complemented and reinforced one another, with the demographic aspects fundamental to their effects.

Starting with the geographical extension of the global market economy, the multiplication of the labour force by three to four times almost entirely consisted of people prepared to work for wages far below norms in advanced countries, while being in many instances – especially in the old Comecon east bloc – quite technical and highly skilled. Amongst the consequences of such a dramatic insertion of low-paid workers were:

- much-increased supply of labour tending to push down wages
- capital assets per worker much reduced
- scarcity of capital assets and cheap labour both boosting profits
- existing capital assets increased in value both through higher profits and a greater multiple of profits by stock market prices
- fixed investment booming in response.

In a pure free-market world, the working-out of these forces would be aided by:

- free trade in goods
- free trade in services
- free movement of capital
- free movement of labour – i.e. migration.

Before 1990, successive rounds of trade liberalisation boosted world trade way beyond the growth of output and incomes, with the latter also much enhanced by freer trade. Agriculture was a notable exception to the freeing of trade, and its natural decline in an era of rising incomes was therefore exacerbated. Moreover, both the volume growth of developing countries' output and the prices they could command have been continuously held back by advanced countries' restrictions on agricultural imports. This has slowed the global tendency towards more equal income distribution, despite poorer countries' faster growth for most of the period since 1990.

International trade in services remained limited, though it developed in tourism, and in finance after the collapse of the Bretton Woods-fixed exchange-rate system in 1970–73. The Thatcher–Reagan accession in 1979–80 progressively freed capital movements, but some restrictions remained. Nonetheless, of the four freedoms listed above, capital flows have probably been the freest.

Migration has been significant, but only a major factor since World War II in the US. The dissolution of colonial regimes by Britain and France, and employment of Turks and others in Germany from the 1950s onward have had significant cumulative effects. This has started to matter politically, just as many advanced countries confront the consequences of declining indigenous populations. Much of this shift is within countries as poor people seek a better life elsewhere – especially in China. Central-eastern Europe has recently seen major migration to richer 'old EU' countries.

The radically new element in terms of migration is the flight from the Middle East (broadly defined to reach from the Maghreb to Afghanistan) and 'Africa proper' (i.e. sub-Saharan, even if the migrants attempt to reach Europe via the Maghreb). These are populations that are certainly not declining, and coping with this flux will be a major test of European countries, as it has the potential, economically, to offset weakness of indigenous demographics while being socially disruptive.

Under the 'Washington consensus' in the 1990s, the chief freedom that advanced was the flow of capital. With tariffs already fairly low in the advanced world, and labour costs spectacularly lower in the newly emerging Eurasian powers, trade boomed without the need for additional policy liberalisation. China liberalised its own import restrictions, hugely benefiting its rapid integration into world trade, with soaring export volumes, especially after the major 1994 devaluation made the currency highly competitive.

India was a lot less enlightened in the manufacturing field, though conditions vary a lot between the different Indian states, but in the Bangalore-based hi-tech boom India burst into world trade in services on the basis of its low costs, which in so many sectors are either unsuitable for international trade (e.g. haircuts, restaurants) or subject to huge non-tariff barriers (e.g. law and medicine).

The mismatch between plentiful cheap labour in emerging Eurasia and large volumes of financial capital in the advanced countries was a natural incentive for capital flows into low-wage countries – and/or labour flows migrating in the opposite direction. This is where cultural and political factors become central.

As a purely economic matter, the most efficient way to raise the income of low-wage people is their migration to an advanced country (or region). That way, education in the techniques and customs of an advanced economy is quickest. Moreover, the additional capital needed for the extra people to be employed is most effectively achieved by 'bolting on' to existing successful operating capacities, rather than some 'green-field' expansion in a new environment that the expatriate managers may not find so easy to handle as their familiar home territory.

Free movement of labour is, however, the freedom that meets the most resistance. This was evident well before the Brexit and Trump votes, though they have made the point crystal clear. Free movement of labour within the original EU, before and after its extensions to include Britain, Scandinavia, Spain, etc., was readily accepted largely because there were fewer massive disparities of income that would provoke major migration flows. While German employment of Italian labour in the 1950s was an exception, Germany was at that stage still in ultra-docile mode, post-World War II.

With EU entry of the low-income east bloc countries, fifty years later in 2004, the threat of a wave of migration led to a seven-year moratorium on their free movement into the old EU countries. Ironically, this was waived by Britain (and also by Ireland and Sweden). When the moratorium ran out in 2011, Germany's fear of demographic decline was vivid enough to make an influx of fresh labour attractive – and so it has proved for German business profits and economic growth, though not so much for the standard of living of the average German.

Resistance to immigration means the bulk of the globalisation effect has not been in labour migration, but in rapid export growth from developing economies, most spectacularly China, and flows of amoral and culturally neutral capital. Foreign direct investment (FDI) flows are the most natural expression of this, both transferring technology to developing economies and taking advantage of cheaper labour for the less sophisticated tasks. But portfolio capital flows are larger than FDI, even in equity markets taken alone.

But this is where the savings glut introduced what seem like unnatural distortions to the global flow of funds. In the classical scheme of globalisation, rich countries have an excess of savings, which they use to take advantage of investment opportunities in poor (or poorer) countries. The model was the pre-World War I wave of globalisation (1880–1914). Britain had a current account surplus typically 10% of national income and financed development all over the globe (not just in the Commonwealth and empire, but also the US, Latin America, etc.).

Over the past quarter-century, and increasingly since 2000, it has not been like that. For a variety of reasons Asian developing economies, especially the Tigers and then China – as in the original savings-glut country, Japan – have had savings well in excess of their investment needs, and even more in excess of reasonable levels of investment, as all these countries have a tendency toward wasteful capex (technically, low productivity of capital). For reasons arising from imbalances in the euro area (see Chapter 2) a huge excess of saving over needed investment developed in the early years of the century. This led to a savings glut in Germany and the countries round Germany (Scandinavia, Benelux and Switzerland–Austria), whose combined economies equal Germany's.

Meanwhile, the richest country in the world, the USA, has both a relatively low investment rate – a tribute to the high productivity of capital bequeathed by its excellent financial system – and an even lower national savings rate. Imbalances between the US on the one hand, and Japan and German-centred Europe on the other, may lead to arguments about their respective policies, capacity to make use of capital, etc. But the spectacle of US consumers being financed in their habits by cheap money and cheap goods from the likes of China was and is decidedly odd, arguably perverse.

The high rate of saving in developing Asia may well suit those countries for a variety of reasons. But this inversion of the natural order was aptly christened 'uphill capital flows' by my former colleague Brian Reading as long ago as 1996, enabling him to forecast the Asian crisis that ensued a year later. Similarly, the much greater and rapidly growing Eurasian savings glut in the 2004–6 period underpinned my forecast of the financial crisis in *The Bill from the China Shop*.

For all the peculiarity of the uphill capital flows from emerging Asian economies to the US, one result of their high saving was easy, low-cost financing of huge volumes of investment in emerging economies in the post-1990 'golden era' of globalisation leading up to the financial crisis. Aside from the lurch into the crisis itself, the problems that this easy period of globalisation have bequeathed include:

- slow growth of real (and nominal) incomes in advanced countries since the crisis – exacerbated by the continued savings glut
- interaction of hi-tech with this slippage of business away from advanced economies to chisel further at real wage incomes
- the 'left-behinds' in such places as Mexico and Africa – fully aware thanks to hi-tech of what they are missing – beginning to say 'we want some of that too', and getting ready to do 'whatever it takes' (in Mario Draghi's famous phrase) to get it, even at the risk of drowning in the Mediterranean.

2

What is a savings glut?

Why refer to a glut of savings rather than simply to a deficiency of demand (as that is what it is)? The use of the phrase 'savings glut' goes beyond the cyclical vagaries of demand to highlight a fixed behavioural tendency of certain nations (sometimes embodied in economic policy) or groups within nations, for reasons specific to them.

So the style of macro-economics advanced here is 'Austrian'. This refers to economics that analyses what happens when classical theory (i.e. monetarism and a fully competitive supply side) is distorted or even invalidated by rigid habits of behaviour, or policy or history, so that adjustments indicated by the classical model are not made. (By this definition, Keynesian theory could be regarded as a special case of Austrian economics, rigidities being the 'zero lower bound' on interest rates and little or no downward flexibility of nominal wages.)

The use of the word 'glut' is relative. On a global, worldwide basis, saving and investment are equal, after the event, by definition. (For a country, gross national savings equal gross national income minus consumption – private plus government – plus net lending abroad. Investment equals total spending minus consumption. But as gross national income and total spending are identical – subject to measurement errors – the difference between a country's saving and investment is the net lending abroad. As globally, such net lending is zero, so globally, gross saving equals investment.)

Figure 1 **Gross world saving**
% of GDP (GWP)

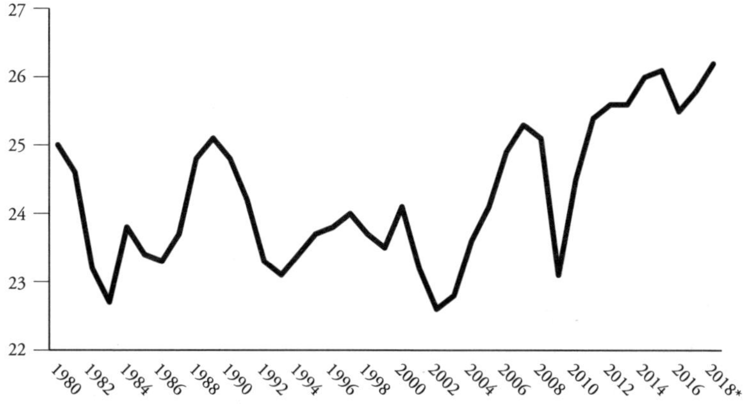

*IMF forecast for 2018
Sources: IMF, TS Lombard, author

Savings can only be called excessive – i.e. a glut – relative to investment opportunities or needs. And that phrase means either (for most capex) what is profitable, relative to the risks involved, or in a few instances capital spending that has to be done to permit proper operation of the economy or society. This latter concept is probably best expressed by saying that the return on investment in such deep infrastructure can be expected to be lower than in ordinary business. (For example, government-financed capex may show a return on capital measured by costs to people if it is not undertaken, rather than as a return to the entity actually doing the capex.)

As it happens, the past few years, as well as pre-crisis 2007, saw record rates of world saving. But the savings glut, proven to exist by prolonged low real and nominal interest rates (see below), may be at least partly a result of falling investment needs owing to slower world population growth.

Much of the need for investment is to cater for the needs of an increase in the total number of people, or in important subgroups such as the working population. This is so-called 'extensive' investment, as opposed to 'intensive' capex that is done to raise the productivity of the economy – or 'maintenance' capex, which is self-explanatory. (In practice, these different forms of capex often overlap.) If population growth falls, the amount of extensive capex that will achieve a given rate of profitability declines. Such a declining need for investment over time could cause a formerly appropriate rate of saving to become excessive; this would be a savings glut, even if the world's savings rate remained unchanged.

Where is the savings glut in the world today? The four chief elements are Japan, certain non-Chinese Asian 'Tigers', German-centred Europe, and China – in historical order as to when they became savings gluttons, not in order of size.

Japan's private sector has saved far more than it needs to invest (even at the low rates of return prevailing there) for decades. It is the original savings glutton, dating at least from the 1970s. Private savings for the past quarter-century have been more than 25% of output, often close to 30%. The Asian Tigers were mauled by the International Monetary Fund – largely protective of Western banks – during the 1997–8 Asian crisis. Their response was 'never again'. So they built up huge reserves via large trade surpluses based on undervalued currencies and export-led growth.

German-centred Europe became artificially undervalued from 1999 onward owing to being yoked together in the euro with inflationary Mediterranean Europe. By 2007, savings exceeded investment rates by an average 7% of GDP, and surplus savings have persisted ever since. Lastly China, cutting back its overheated domestic demand in 2005–7, raised its national savings rate to an extraordinary 50% of GDP by 2007. It remained at that level until 2015.

The historical context of the savings glut starts with the German *Wirtschaftswunder* ('economic miracle') of the 1950s. Germany restored its post-world-war economy to parity with Britain by about 1960 (though not with America) by pursuing a policy of high savings and export-led growth. This was helped by Germany becoming increasingly undervalued owing to its restrained labour costs within the Bretton Woods system of fixed exchange rates.

Japan followed Germany down this road from the mid-1950s onward. Between them they destroyed the theory of development economics then current, which placed the emphasis on national autonomy through import substitution. That theory had the drawback that countries would end up with a host of small-scale industries, each one uncompetitive with the world's best. India, for example, followed the autonomy route for more than thirty years after independence in 1947, and this contributed mightily to its feeble growth performance until the late 1970s, since reversed by the 'green revolution', and after 1991, economic liberalisation.

Germany's export-led growth enabled it to develop industries competitive on a world scale, and its output grew at about 10% a year in the 1950s, as did Japan's from the mid-1950s until the first oil crisis in 1973. Their example was followed by Korea in the 1970s, by the Asian Tigers generally in the 1980s, and finally by China in the twenty years running up to the financial crisis of 2008, and then to its growth peak in 2011.

For each such country or region taken individually the policy made sense. But for the entire group of these countries it became subject to the 'fallacy of composition': the incorrect belief that something that is good or right for individuals in a group is necessarily good or right for the whole group.

Two points underpin the fallacy of composition in this situation. They are crucial to understanding the consequences of this focus on export-led growth. First, the world trade balance is by definition nil. For every surplus there has to be a corresponding deficit. (The world is not yet in a position to export to the Moon, or Mars!) As the range of countries seeking export-led growth broadened, other countries found it harder to achieve good economic results while running the corresponding deficits.

Second, the high savings rates in savings-glut countries, often amongst the world's fastest-growing, led increasingly to a rising global rate of saving. But globally, saving equals investment by definition. And the world simply did not need a rising investment rate. So the forced deployment of this unneeded capital led to falling returns on investment and low nominal and real interest rates. The real-world resolution of all this has been complex and interactive, but the essence of it is that the investment undertaken is of lower quality – with an increasing element of waste and misallocation of resources, sapping long-run growth potential.

The impulse to save is largely independent of the impulse to invest. People do not save with the thought that they have some high-yield project they want to finance. Saving by people (as opposed to businesses) is mostly driven by fear, not greed. They may be worried about getting old, getting sick, losing their job – or simply wanting a holiday (the minor 'greed' element). Saving by businesses takes the form of depreciation (ostensibly to finance replacement capex) and retained profits. This may just reflect prior capex and the state of the economy, though strong retained profit can also spur investment, using up a business's own savings, and perhaps other people's as well.

The sum of private savings can be cut by the government, if its current spending exceeds its tax and other revenues, and vice versa. (This is not the same as the budget deficit, or borrowing requirement, as that generally adds in the effect of government capex and capital taxes and transfers.) The sources of the national savings rate in a country are complex.

To name obvious cases, investment may be done by

- businesses pursuing profit opportunities, or suffering supply bottlenecks through strong demand that raises capacity utilisation
- households wanting better accommodation or

- governments providing needed infrastructure.

The linkage of desired investment to the propensity to save is weak at best.

If the desire to save exceeds the desire to invest, the links between the two – the return on capital and/or the rate of interest – will fall, and vice versa. The most useful concept of the rate of interest (corresponding to the return on capital in a business or infrastructure project) is the so-called 'real' rate of interest: the actual (called 'nominal') rate minus inflation. In the explosion of financial activity in 2004–7, real rates of interest remained below long-term average levels – clear evidence that the upsurge of saving was the driving force, and the investment activity the response. The increase of waste and misallocation needed no further proof than the US sub-prime crisis, and the lurch into debt crises of the UK, Ireland and Mediterranean countries.

Figure 2 **Japanese private saving**
% of GDP

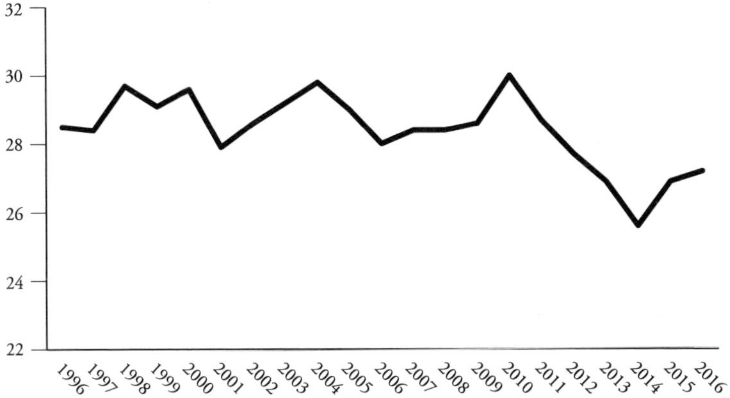

Sources: Japanese SNA, TS Lombard, author

Figure 3 **Japanese and Asian 'Tigers'**
Current-account balance

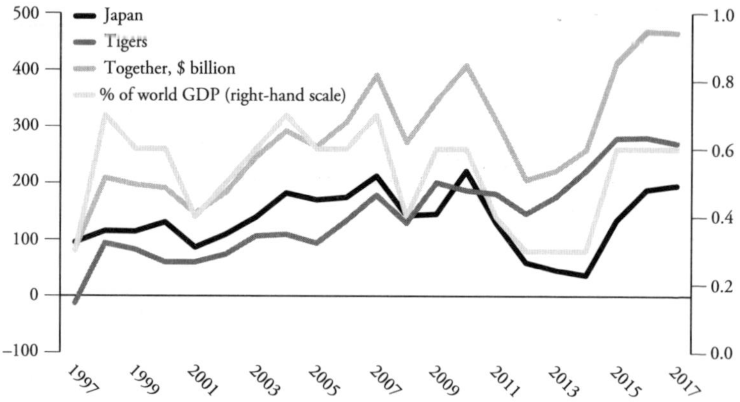

Sources: IMF, TS Lombard, author

The Asian crisis was the beginning of the Eurasian savings glut, if one accepts that Japanese savings had been excessive for several decades.

The crisis countries were brutally punished by the IMF, acting effectively as agents for the global banking system, and emerged from the crisis in 1999 determined never again to be caught out financially. So they saved heavily, building up huge surpluses and foreign exchange reserves – effectively exporting capital to the US.

Next, after 2002, came the effects of the euro. There the imbalances were largely internal until the financial crisis. The internal imbalances concerned both relative costs and interest rates. Mediterranean Europe and Ireland had faster growth and inflation than German-centred Europe. They should have had higher interest rates too; but the 'one size fits all' interest rate ('one size fits none' says it better) led to gross over-investment in these countries, matching or even outweighing their soaring trade deficits. A major build-up of saving in Germany and the surrounding countries of north-central

Figure 4 **EA current account balances**
$ billion

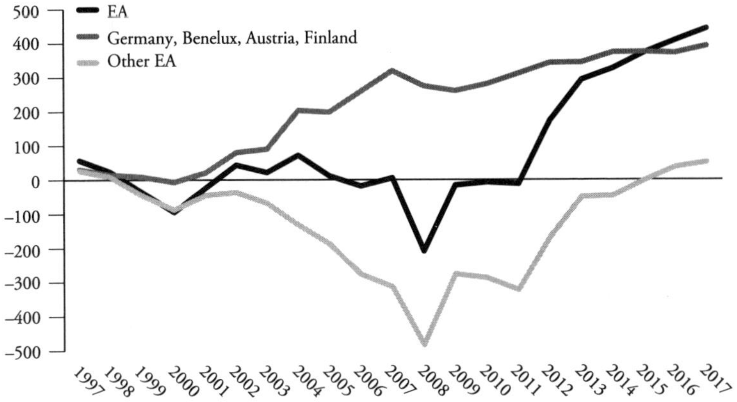

Sources: IMF, TS Lombard, author

Europe was matched by a shift into large debt-financed deficits in Mediterranean Europe and Ireland. The UK too was in the deficit group.

The dangerous distortions imposed by the euro system are described in Chapter 14. A key point is that the policies eventually adopted to cope with the 2010–13 euro crisis were similar to the 1997–8 Asian crisis impositions, in that they were basically designed to protect lending banks. But there was an added twist: not only was default largely forbidden, but so was devaluation – by the very nature of the euro system – so that massive deflation of demand was all that was left. As a result, the eurozone, notably the countries round Germany, is now the largest savings glutton in the world. With the former deficit countries forced back to current account balance, large surpluses in German-centred Europe are no longer offset within the EA, as they were until 2008.

Last but very far from least into the savings-glut camp came China, with an exploding rate of surplus and capital export from

Figure 5 **Shares of Chinese GDP**
%

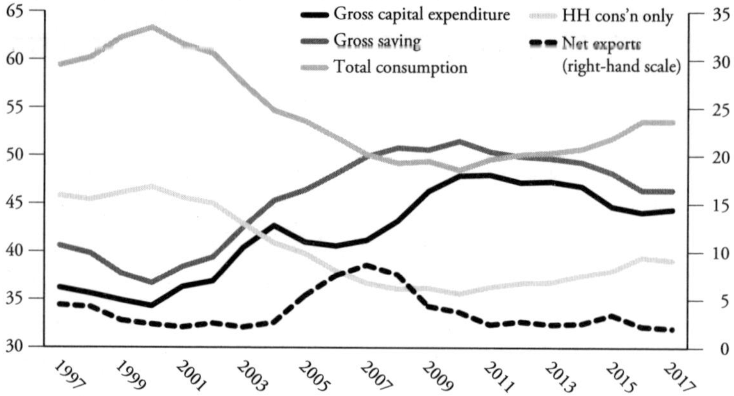

Sources: CEIC, TS Lombard, author

2005 onward. By 2007 its national savings rate was half of total output (gross domestic product, GDP), and the current account surplus was 9%. With China's economy approaching the US in size, this meant that China and the Tigers combined were accounting for about half the current-account surplus of savings-glut countries – and were busily funding, at relatively low rates of return, many much richer countries. Moreover, the combined weight of surpluses in the savings glut – including Japan and German-centred Europe as well – was requiring deficits on the rest of the world that were beyond their capacity.

A structural or behavioural tendency to save too much in a group of countries, as described here, can lead to only a limited variety of effects or responses:

1. **Higher private investment.** For investment to be higher than it would be otherwise, and use up the excess saving, the required rate of return on new assets has to be driven down. Such a

lower rate of return would be a natural thing to expect if the supply of funds (saving) is boosted. In pre-Keynesian, classical economics, this is the normal, orthodox response. One means by which a strong flow of saving will achieve this is by pulling up the price of existing stocks and shares, effectively lowering their yield, i.e. the rate of return to new investors. The higher price of existing stocks and shares thus encourages firms to invest and sell shares to investors. This can be regarded either as creating assets more highly valued in the stock market than their cost, or simply as creating assets that can be sold at a lower rate of return than their actual yield – these two descriptions are economically and financially equivalent. In the pre-crisis US the chief effect of this was the sub-prime mortgage-financed housing bubble, with similar activities in Britain, Ireland, Spain, Portugal and Australia.

2. **Lower private savings.** Without any changes in public policy, a lower rate of return might also (on reasonable assumptions) be expected to lessen the attraction of private saving, whether in the glut countries or (more likely) elsewhere. Again this is a natural classical response. It applied in pre-crisis America, but not in many other countries. Many people save and buy interest-paying assets (e.g. bonds or bank accounts) to provide a pension. For them, a lower real rate of interest may cut the accumulation of value in their pension fund, forcing them to save *more* – not *less*, as classical theory would indicate – to reach a given post-retirement income.
3. **Easier monetary policy.** Easier monetary policy in non-glut countries could use up excess savings in a number of ways. First, by validating and promoting a lower rate of interest (the fundamental cost of capital) it could induce a combination of higher investment and (perhaps) lower savings, provoking via policy the two responses described above. Secondly, if the economy were below full employment (whether or not caused by the weak

demand implicit in a savings glut) it could induce growth in domestic demand and net imports.

4. **Easier fiscal policy.** Government can directly dis-save or invest, offsetting the savings glut, by shifting toward deficit financing. (This was Keynes's last-resort remedy in the Depression, and the first-resort remedy of 'Keynesians' for any slowdown since 1945.) This was partly done pre-crisis in the US and UK, and has been a long-standing, if reluctant, resort in Japan.
5. **Depression of demand, income and output.** Lastly, if the responses above occur on an insufficient scale, the potential savings glut will express itself as global demand weakness, lowering output and incomes to the level where the savings out of such income are no longer higher than investment. The investment in such scenarios generally includes a large measure of unwanted inventory, as sales falling short of businessmen's expectations. This inventory hangover lowers future demand – i.e. raises further the potential savings surplus. Equally, so can lower investment in response to weaker demand and output. Thus, demand, income and output can go into a downward spiral.

3

Financial crisis as excess saving boosts debts

The run-up to the crisis in 2003–7 saw the first three of these responses to the savings glut that was itself 'on the move' – in Japan, north-central Europe and finally China. In Japan the long-standing excess of *private* saving over investment needs changed little. But the counterpart deficit shifted from government to foreigners. The budget deficit, 7¾% of GDP in 2002, was tightened sharply, down to 1½–2% in 2006–7, raising the *national* savings rate by nearly three percentage points of GDP. In parallel with the fiscal tightening, monetary policy was kept loose; the zero-interest-rate policy (ZIRP) was kept in place despite strong world growth, and above-trend growth in Japan itself, though prices remained stable. ZIRP led to depreciation of the yen. Combined with strong growth elsewhere, this swelled Japan's trade surplus, giving the country an overseas surplus as the offset for its excessive private saving, replacing the previous budget deficit.

The emergence of the surplus in north-central Europe, centred on Germany, was a by-product of the uniform exchange rate in the euro area interacting with different growth and inflation rates amongst the various countries in the EA. These differences were exacerbated by the euro. The common interest rate, too high for Germany and France, too low for Italy and Spain, overstimulated the latter while restraining the former – reinforced in Germany's case by extremely tight fiscal restraint in 2002–5. So the German surplus grew rapidly – as did those of Scandinavia, Benelux and Switzerland-Austria – while Mediterranean deficits widened to match. Europe was thus a smaller version of the global story.

German-centred Europe's savings glut held down interest rates despite unaffordable debt build-ups in the counterpart 'peripheral' deficit countries, Mediterranean Europe and Ireland. Thus the euro system prolonged the build-up of debt so that its overshoot was greater. The eventual crisis was more intense than it would have been if interest rate increases had soared, to curb the debt bubble earlier. This too is a regional version of the global story, in which credulous international capital flows kept unsustainable behaviour going for longer.

In China, the national savings rate had veered around 40% of GDP from the late 1980s to early this century. By 2007 it had mounted to 50% of GDP, higher than any rate in recorded economic history. Undervaluation of the currency in a world trade boom caused business profits to boom, with little distribution to consumers. Households continued their very high rate of saving, reflecting long-standing traditions, lack of social security or health services, and insecurity arising from the one-child policy instituted in 1980. Household income was falling relative to GDP. But the latter's growth averaging more than 10% in this period left room for consumer spending to grow at 7% in real terms, while household income growth in-between these two rates allowed greater saving.

The common strategy of savings-glut countries, whether in Japan, the Asian Tigers, north-central Europe or China, was to lay off excessive saving by means of undervalued currencies (or countries in the euro system) to generate current account surpluses, exporting the excess capital. In the world at large, however, overvalued currencies (or countries) had to be equivalent to the undervalued ones – the world can neither be overvalued nor undervalued vis-à-vis itself. And it seems to have to be frequently and regularly pointed

Figure 6 **World gross saving and real US Treasury yields**

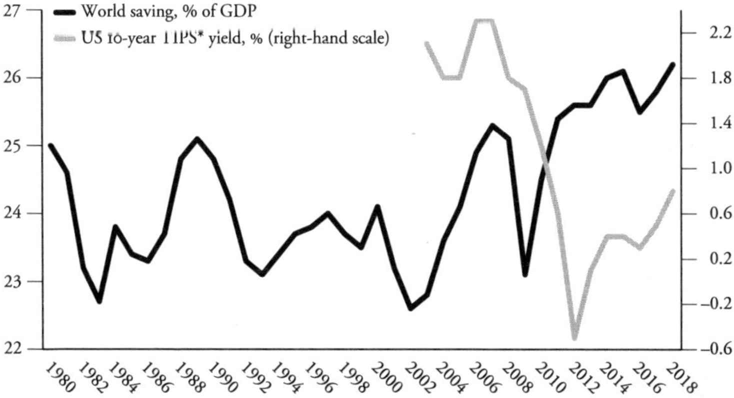

*Treasury Inflation-Protected Securities.
Sources: IMF, TS Lombard, author

out that the world cannot have either a surplus or a deficit with itself. For every country running a surplus there has to be an equal deficit somewhere else. Yet by the 2005–7 period, the savings glut countries just listed comprised more than 30% of world GDP.

Which country's real exchange rate was most conspicuously buoyed up pre-crisis by this undervaluation of the savings gluttons? Obviously, the United States, though also Britain and much of Mediterranean Europe. The cheap-FX, export-led strategy of savings gluttons was transparently based on treating the US as the market of first resort – as it had been through successive waves of trade liberalisation since Germany's 1950s *Wirtschaftswunder*. Nor was the US a reluctant partner in this imbalance: US consumers were offered cheap goods and cheap money to buy them with – it would have been rude to refuse.

The key point is that in contrast to previous US debt-driven booms, e.g. 1988–90's 'high-leverage' boom, excessive saving elsewhere in the world kept real interest rates low. As the chart above shows, in the boom period, 2004–7, the real yield of ten-year US Treasuries averaged 2%, despite its long run (100-year) average being 2½%. Real yields stayed so low despite the extravagant excesses of both the housing debt run-up and the financial sector's vast expansion of assets and liabilities. This is the clearest evidence that it was excessive saving that enabled the bubble to continue so dangerously long and far.

Pre-crisis America adopted the first three responses to the low interest rates arising from the spate of world savings. Private investment was higher, notably in wasteful housing, whose value crashed after the sub-prime crisis. Private savings fell; though business saving was sustained by the bubble-boosting domestic activity, the personal savings rate fell sharply. And monetary policy was easy.

While Mr Greenspan's rhetoric at the Fed was Panglossian, it is hard to see what else he could have done in 2003–7. Real growth was respectable, at just under 3%, but not strong by US upswing standards. Inflation averaged less than 3%, only a little over 2% excluding booming oil prices. A tighter monetary policy to cut back on the financial machinations that led to the sub-prime crisis would have seemed perverse. It would have clearly contradicted the Fed's mandate – to foster employment as well as low inflation – and might well have led to Congressional curbs on the Fed.

While the Fed's chief instrument, the federal funds rate, has exceeded inflation by an average of just under 2% since the 1950s, after the 2001 (non-)'recession' it did not rise to match inflation until 2005, and reached 2% above it only at the peak of the bubble in 2006–7. While this writer and some others were forecasting a US household debt crisis in 2006–7, for most economists, let alone politicians and others closely interested, sub-prime travails came out of the blue. Mr Greenspan returning real short-term US rates back to their long-run average seemed a perfectly acceptable response to a maturing economic cycle.

Mr Bernanke, Fed chairman from spring 2006, is more culpable.

He had named the savings glut in March 2005, though my original piece on the concept was in September 2004. He should have seen that US borrowing to offset the excess savings of others might drive private debt to unaffordable levels, provoking crisis.

4

Savings glut hobbles recovery

While the imbalances summarised as the savings glut were the underlying economic cause of the crisis, it was exacerbated by the extravagant and sometimes illegal carnival of financial excess. But by the middle of 2009 it was clear what was needed to permit a healthy world recovery from the crisis, and also fairly clear that the needed rebalancing would not occur.

The crisis was (of course) a debt crisis, and in response to any debt crisis the debtors need to save more and spend less. It follows that in the US, the UK, Ireland and Mediterranean Europe a cutback in consumption would follow, once the immediate danger of a lapse into depression had been averted by means of fiscal stimulus. If the world was to enjoy a healthy recovery, therefore, other countries, notably the savings gluttons, would need to consume more – i.e. save less. Broadly speaking, taking the three major countries concerned, Japan would have but could not, Germany could have but would not, while China understood the need for more spending and was able to do it, but did it in the wrong way, with damaging consequences from 2012 onwards.

Germany's attitude was especially important, since its key role in the destructive policies to preserve the euro in the systemic crisis of 2010–13 made the whole adjustment process in Mediterranean Europe and Ireland slower and dramatically painful. The broad description of what it takes to deal with a debt crisis is what my former colleague Brian Reading called the '3 Ds'. These are devaluation, deflation (of demand, not necessarily prices) and default.

The key point is that omission of any one of the three 'D's means over-reliance on the others, making adjustment slower and more painful. To take an example from the Asian crisis, the bail-out imposed on Korea by the IMF did not allow for any default, even though much of the lending to countries in the run-up to that crisis was clearly badly judged, and therefore lenders deserved some of the blame for the resulting debacle. When banks make rotten loans it is not just the borrowers who should suffer.

But the IMF was (and is) dominated by international banking interests, and only the first two 'D's, devaluation and deflation, were in its programme. As a result, the devaluation was deeper than it might have been, and the demand deflation more painful. Ironically, as Korea emerged from the process saying 'never again', the lesson it learnt was to be in huge overseas surplus, making the Asian Tigers the first savings gluttons after Japan – with China, a highly interested nearby observer, learning the same lesson. So one crisis knocked on to the next, ten years later.

In the immediate aftermath of the financial crisis, the US effectively adopted all three of the 'D's, once the 2009 fiscal stimulus had helped prevent the severe recession turning into a prolonged depression. (This still seems quite likely to have happened without the emergency programme.) As a result of its enlightened policies, US growth since 2007's pre-crisis peak has been the best of the major advanced countries, better than Germany and Japan, which had no debt crisis.

The deflation aspect of US policy is shown by its cyclically adjusted budget deficit falling from more than 10% of GDP in 2009 and 2010 to less than 4% three years later, in 2013. The devaluation arose because monetary easing was adopted with a vengeance, sending the US real exchange rate down to historically low levels by

2011. As for default, it occurred in the crisis itself: huge mortgage defaults were the cause of the crisis, though much of the pain was transferred to taxpayers via bailouts of the banks.

The contrast is clear between the US on the one hand, and the UK and Mediterranean Europe on the other. In the UK, mortgage defaults were largely avoided, as UK mortgages mostly bear floating interest rates, so their monthly cost was sharply reduced as interest rates fell to zero. While households were kept afloat by this, the prevalence of 'zombie' households with negative equity inhibited recovery as confidence remained low while savings rates were high.

Devaluation occurred in that the pound's real exchange rate plunged. But it plunged from major overvaluation in the 1997–2007 period, so that it never fell to a level as competitive as the dollar under easy money. And one result was that the deflation of domestic demand by fiscal tightening, although less than in the euro area, inhibited recovery, which did not catch up with Germany's until 2014–15. Like Germany, Britain's recovery suffered from the euro crisis, which both held down exports and total activity. It also helped to prevent the needed scale of devaluation, as continental flight money flowed in.

For heavily indebted Mediterranean Europe, the mechanisms of the euro system proved a disaster in the aftermath of the financial crisis. This was not just a function of the euro's very existence – though prevention of devaluation by the countries that needed it was probably the single largest obstacle to effective adjustment. But the existence of the EA, and the obvious relevance of currency inflexibility to any possible adjustment, meant that the EA was the vehicle through which the question of default was also decided.

The decisions by Mrs Merkel and Mr Sarkozy in 2010–11 were clear: no write-offs of cross-border loans, minimal mutual help for the countries in trouble, and requirement to subscribe to the principle of the original, 1998 'Stability and Growth Pact' (SGP) – itself widely ignored by its propagator Germany when it suited it in 2001–5. Ironically, Spain, a chief victim of the euro crisis, ran average budget *surpluses* of 1% of output in 2003–7, while Germany, principal EA disciplinarian, averaged *deficits* of 2½%. Fiscal virtue did not protect Spain from the debt crisis – and neither was fiscal vice the major cause of it. (That, for Spain, was the euro itself.)

Deprived of both devaluation and default, EA debt-crisis countries were left with deflation alone as a cure – and by itself deflation tended to make matters worse. A debt crisis by definition refers to the relation of debt to the income that can pay the interest and ultimately repay the loan. Deflation of demand lowers income, in a subdued global context and with no devaluation to provide compensating stimulus.

Reduced income makes any given debt burden less affordable – a debt crisis is therefore made *worse* by deflation without the salve of either devaluation or default. That sustained EA recovery has been possible since 2013 is owed to the adoption of ultra-easy monetary policies by the European Central Bank in 2014–15, presaged by its president, Mario Draghi, talking the euro down hard from mid-2014. More of that below, but Draghi's policy was in essence to devalue, and thus export the EA's deflation to the rest of the world, notably its largest trading partner, Britain.

What the EA authorities claimed to be trying to achieve was 'internal devaluation' in the debtor countries. In reality, of course, it was the exposure of German and French banks to the EA debt-crisis countries that was decisive in the proscription of default. At the cost of six years with unemployment over 20%, peaking at 27% and averaging 23%, Spain has bludgeoned its labour costs down. As it is now just below 20%, the 80%-plus of the labour force now in work is cost-competitive, helped, of course, by the ECB's cheap-euro policies since 2014.

Spain's GDP in 2017 is finally above its pre-crisis peak, and growing fast. Greece, on the other hand, where unemployment was similar to Spain's, lost more than a quarter of its output by 2013 under the auspices of EA policies, and has flat-lined since without recovery. Modest recovery is now likely, owing to tourism in so much of the rest of the Mediterranean being blighted by dictatorship and war. In terms of broad human welfare, both experiences have been disastrous.

The behaviour of the savings-glut countries was fundamental to the difficulties of turning round the debt crises, and the sluggish world recovery. Japan's private sector continued to save nearly 30% of output, for most of the time exceeding its capital spending by a massive 9% of output. The offset to this financial surplus by pre-crisis 2007 had been shifted away to overseas surpluses from the large budget deficits of 1998–2002. But the collapse of exports in the crisis, the sudden recovery of the yen, and the slump of private capital spending that increased the private financial surplus meant that by 2012 the current account surplus was down to 1% of output and the budget deficit was up to 8–9%.

Over the long run the necessity for Japanese budget deficits to average 6% of output (see Chapter 12) causes rising public debt that constantly leads to political attempts to cut the deficit. This works alongside the private savings surplus to weaken the economy. Japan's private surplus thus creates a permanent trend towards debt problems – it is a structural feature of the economy that is beyond the reach of either Keynesian or monetarist demand management.

While Japan, absent profound structural reforms, could not and still cannot contribute domestic demand, in particular consumption, to world recovery, Germany simply *would not* in the post-crisis period, even though it could have. At the very peak of the crisis and recession in mid-2009, Germany amended the constitution to mandate balanced budgets. The recession effects led to a cyclically adjusted budget deficit of 3¼% of output in 2010, but this was cut to nil by 2013. The German private sector's surplus of 7–8% of output expressed itself entirely in 2007's current account surplus of 7%. This has shifted upward from 2013 onward to more than 8%.

A key point is that the fixed exchange rates within the euro system, combined with Germany's inflation being less than in Mediterranean Europe, ensured that the euro's exchange rate tended (and tends) to be too high for the latter and overly competitive for Germany. So Germany gained market share from its EA 'partners' while at the same time deflating its own domestic demand through budget austerity, in both respects making debtor countries' recovery harder to achieve.

To cap off the damage caused by the lack of adequate domestic demand in Japan and German-centred Europe, these countries then effectively embarked on aggressive, beggar-my-neighbour competitive devaluations, undoing the newly acquired (and badly needed) US competitiveness of 2011–13. Japan had two rounds of major devaluation, from late 2012 to spring 2013, and then in the year from mid-2014. The EA joined in the devaluation game with its ultra-easy money from autumn 2014, causing a slump in the euro. If the story had ended there, the result could have been a fresh global recession – or at least slowdown.

The fallacy of too much reliance on monetary policy and particularly quantitative easing (QE) to rescue the world economy is analysed in Chapter 8. The key point for this narrative is that monetary policy is unlikely to provide a cure for problems arising from structural rigidities. Thus, 2008–12 QE in America and Britain genuinely improved the world situation by rebalancing the dollar to a lower level, undoing some of the damage from the pre-crisis imbalances, not least because the US and UK are closer to being pure market economies than others. By contrast, the beggar-my-neighbour response from Japan and the EA simply attempted to grab a bigger share of world demand, without making any contribution to its increase.

In the event, the accumulation of deflationary forces, with China also enjoying slower growth from 2012 onward, led to a collapse of oil and other energy and commodity prices, especially in late 2014.

The surpluses of oil and commodity countries had remained high, though the cyclical price peak was in 2011, and this was in effect a cyclical element of savings glut, adding to the effects of the structural glut countries already described. The collapse of oil and commodity prices brought great benefits to world consumers that outweighed the cutback of the producers', and producing countries', spending. So the global effect was net stimulus – but the world had to wait.

The net stimulus from cheaper oil and metals was a balance of cuts in demand, coming first, with demand stimulus later. In its initial impact, the collapse in oil prices was simply a redistribution of income from oil producers to oil consumers. Only later did this mean that exploitative parts of the world economy lost value while value-added parts – manufacturing and service – gained income. And the value-added parts have always been inherently more productive than people simply digging holes in the ground to extract the world's resources. So lower prices for using what has always been there yields a net gain for the world economy.

Pain causes quicker reactions than gain. As oil and commodity prices plunged, the response of suffering producers was faster than that of consumers enjoying windfall gains. This was much as in 1986, when plunging oil prices caused a mid-decade slowdown – to the surprise of many analysts expecting a quick reversal of the then-recent oil crisis damage. This time the slowdown was more prolonged, aggravated by Chinese weakness, the sharp rise of the dollar – reflecting the coincidence of the oil-price slump with the aggressive beggar-my-neighbour devaluation of Japan and the eurozone – and by an inventory downswing owing to excessive US stock-building until summer 2014.

It was not just the US and its dollar that were left high and dry by euro-Japanese predation. In contrast with such globally antisocial policies, China, an ongoing savings glutton, had since 2011 combined its ultra-high savings and capex with an appreciating yuan that by spring of 2015 caused it to be 15% or so higher in real terms than in 2010, the last year in which Chinese exports were clearly cost-competitive. The result of grossly excessive and wasteful capex, averaging 47–8% of GDP in the six years 2009–14, and an increasingly uncompetitive exchange rate was a sharp growth slowdown, accompanied by rapid escalation of domestic debt levels. It approached the dimensions of a crisis.

China was seen through by its reserves, just as it had been seen through the Asian crisis in 1997–8 by the undervaluation of its currency. (While the Chinese juggernaut was underestimated in the 1990s, analysts close to the Asian crisis in many cases suggested that the massive Chinese devaluation of 1994 had in fact been a major cause of it, undermining the Asian Tigers.) Chinese reserves fell about $1 trillion from a peak of $4 trillion in 2014 to a low point of $3 trillion in early 2017. Adding a current account surplus of $650 billion over this period means the gross capital outflow was more than $1½ trillion. About $500 billion was used to reduce private sector debts in foreign currency and the remainder represented net private capital outflow: both Chinese people managing to take money out of the country and foreigners withdrawing prior investments.

With a drop of 10% in the real exchange rate between the April 2015 peak and its 2017 trough, even though the real FX rate remained 5% above the 2010 average, the stage was set for a significant Chinese government stimulus during 2016, permitting a rapid recovery of growth while the escalation of debt slowed significantly. China therefore started to recover just as financial market views about the world economy bottomed out, reflecting the temporary US growth slowdown in early 2016. The malignant policies of Japan and the eurozone had made the mid-decade slowdown significantly worse and longer than its 1980s equivalent, when oil prices previously slumped (in their roughly thirty-year cycle). But the benefit of rebalancing the world economy away from excessive energy and commodity prices has started to show through since early 2016.

5

Recovery recovers – but is trend growth slower?

The world has surprised itself with a Houdini-like recovery since early 2016.

The sustained improvement of real consumer incomes arising from the oil price (and other commodity) slump has led to a major revival not just in the US, but also in Europe and China. Not since the 1990s has the world economy had three major locomotives – i.e. economies driven by domestic demand and activity, rather than relying on exports to exploit other countries' domestic demand. The US economy has always been a locomotive in this sense. But before the financial crisis its demand growth was unduly dependent on a run-up of debt, as we have seen. The same was true of the other pre-crisis locomotives: Britain and Ireland, and Mediterranean Europe – so the financial crisis rapidly morphed into the euro crisis.

The US was joined as a locomotive by China from 2009, though its dependence on grotesquely high capex has weakened its economy since the first rush of recovery (2009–11), meaning that the debt-dependence of growth was shifted from the pre-crisis candidates to China (and also Japan – see Chapter 12). But in 2016–17 a new locomotive emerged: continental Europe, and in particular Germany and its surrounding countries. Scandinavia, Holland/Belgium and Switzerland/Austria have aggregate GDP equal to Germany's, so that German-centred north-central Europe is effectively Germany times two. As such it is nearly three times France (and the UK) as an economy, and nearly four times Italy. With Spain also now returned to competitiveness and fast growth, the continental economy (which is significantly more than just the eurozone) has become as strong a locomotive as the US.

Some features of the revived recovery set it apart from previous experience. The good news is that inflation remains very restrained, including wage inflation: major wage hikes in response to falling unemployment are yet to be felt. (This is not an entirely favourable development, of course, as income gains are the chief reason for wanting economic growth, and the current crisis over populism is closely connected to erosion of lower-middle incomes.) Also, the global momentum means that even Chinese demand growth is no longer debt-dependent, meaning this expansion looks sounder than any this century.

The bad news relates to the same phenomenon of falling unemployment. Its decline at a time of quite modest growth by historical standards suggests that the sustainable growth rate – the growth trend, or potential long-run growth rate – is much reduced from the bulk of the post-World War II experience. US real growth as measured has averaged 2.1% since the recovery started in spring 2009, but the rapid decline of unemployment suggests that the long-run 'speed limit' is 1¾% growth. Likewise the eurozone, whose trend growth was already paltry before the financial crisis at 1½%, is now estimated by the OECD to have potential growth of only 1%, though either this is improving or it is simply too low, since the EA has been growing significantly faster recently without much upswing of core inflation. In China the growth trend has inevitably slowed, but as it was well over 10% until 2011, the slippage to about a 6½% trend since then is hardly a worry.

Has trend growth slowed, and if so why?

The degree to which growth has slowed is disputed by analysts who focus on the measurement of output, spending and incomes, especially as regards the effects of innovation after the past twenty years' hi-tech transformation of people's lives. It is becoming increasingly likely that the benefits of hi-tech, both in growth and price reductions, may have been significantly under-measured in the official statistics of growth and inflation. This issue will be covered elsewhere (p. 53).

The slowdown in trend growth as it is currently measured is beyond dispute, though it varies by country. Within the EA average the German trend rate has been improving, and may now be approaching 2%. Though the official OECD estimate is still only 1.3–1.4%, this underestimates the upward influence of major immigration, now supplemented by the influx of refugees. Such near-2% potential growth may only be temporary, but probably still has a few years to run.

While for France the OECD's estimate of 1.3% potential growth could be on the high side, its Spanish estimate of 0.8–0.9% is way too low – growth has averaged 3% in recent years, and while that has induced some inflationary uptick it has certainly not been at a runaway pace. In Italy, on the other hand, the official estimate that trend growth is roughly nil seems correct. Output per head has been until this year's modest revival below the level of 1998, the last year before the euro.

Elsewhere, the leader in decline amongst advanced countries has been, of course, Japan, where the average growth rate has been ¾% a year for twenty years now, dividing into 1% a year for the first ten and ½% over the more recent ten years (and the last five years). A widespread view is that the whole 'Western' world is following in Japan's footsteps – with Japan the first to reach a low but fairly stable growth. As the analysis presented here on Japan, the US, Europe and China makes clear, this idea has no foundation. Japan's decline has unique features, though aspects of the behaviour that has caused it can be found elsewhere.

The UK too has seen a fall in its growth trend. It was estimated at 2½% pre-crisis, and this had come down to 1½% by 2016. OECD estimates show it being further reduced by Brexit, but these estimates are based on 'establishment' hostility to Brexit. Official views about how it will affect growth have so far proved much too pessimistic. The UK case is not only complex because of Brexit, but also indeterminate in advance of the settlement with the EU being finalised. This is well over a year away.

In the US, the growth rate of productivity has slumped over the past dozen years, as the chart below shows. The 7½-year average growth rate largely eliminates the variations caused by the cyclical sensitivity of productivity. The current rate of growth of ¾% has been consistent for several years, as the three-year average shows. With underlying labour-force growth perhaps 1% a year, this suggests the two combined give a potential growth rate of about 1¾%. But long-run falls in average weekly hours, or slower growth of

Figure 7 **US output per hour worked**
Non-farm business, period averages, %

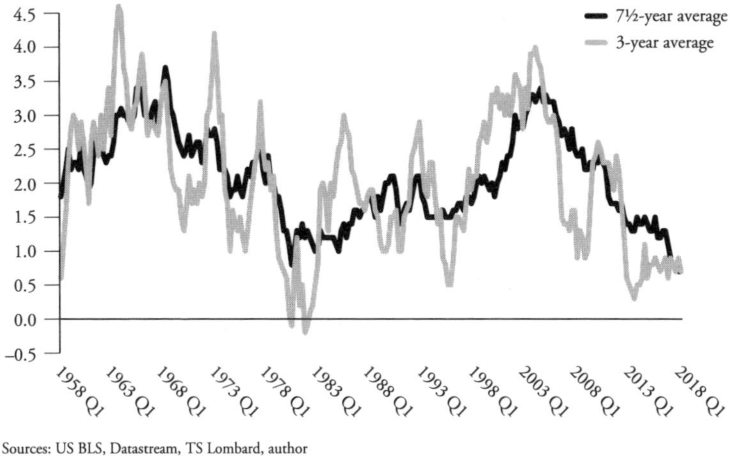

Sources: US BLS, Datastream, TS Lombard, author

productivity in government service than in business, would pull the potential growth rate down further. By comparison, the growth averages in the last forty to fifty years of the twentieth century were 3–3¼%.

It is tempting to suggest that the prevalence of slower trend growth throughout the advanced countries means there is a common cause (or causes). But a number of deviations from past recoveries are relevant to this growth slowdown, with some degree of commonality between countries, but also major differences. Examples of factors that may have contributed include:

1. Slower growth of the net capital stock, despite the gross investment/GDP ratio for the world economy being at a record high, possible reasons for this including:
   a) China's massive capex, a rapidly increasing and low-quality share of the world total, crowding out advanced countries' investment
   b) 'Hysteresis': prolonged post-crisis weakness of demand has depressed capacity utilisation and 'animal spirits' (the appetite for risk) so that the trend level of real output and incomes has been bent down to a lower medium-term growth slope, reducing the need for capital assets
   c) Many countries (e.g. US, UK, Germany) seeing faster expansion than previously of low-income jobs, both dragging down average incomes per employee and also substituting low-income workers for labour-saving capex that would have raised productivity
2. Globalisation
   a) A sharp shift of output and incomes in favour of low-income countries may have contributed to some of the points under (1) above, including obviously (1a) Chinese investment crowding-out, and (1b) hysteresis from slower medium-term growth – though the bulk of the cause of this arose from

the concentration of debt crises in advanced countries rather than emerging markets

b) Increased international labour mobility may have added to the concentration of advanced-country job creation on low-income functions (1c above)

3. Lesser labour mobility in the US (and maybe the UK), where negative or minimal post-crisis housing equity and fear of student debt burdens have restricted the range of many people's job searches
4. Under-measurement of the benefits of hi-tech, either through
   a) Hi-tech benefits not being measured properly as income gains (see p. 53)
   b) The fall in hi-tech prices having been faster than as officially measured
   c) Many benefits of hi-tech being free (e.g. email, Google searches) or
   d) Major hi-tech savings in capex requirements (e.g. online purchases reducing the need for investment in shops).

The chart overleaf shows the growth rate of the real net capital stock of various countries, measured as a seven-year average to minimise cyclical ups and downs – though these are hard to eliminate entirely. In the US, its growth was around 3% until the turn of the century, much in line with real GDP, and it has since declined to 1¼–1½%, a slightly greater fall than that of the growth trend (from 3%-plus to 1½–1¾%). In the US perhaps even more than elsewhere, the progress of hi-tech has saved capital, so this decline may be less important than in other countries.

Unsurprisingly, the greatest fall in the growth of the real net capital stock has been in Japan. It was over 5% until the 1990s, but during the past twenty years has collapsed. So much so that the real capital stock has actually been falling slightly in recent years, and was unchanged in 2017 from 2007. While this may represent hi-tech

Figure 8 **Growth of real net capital stock**
% per annum, 7-year moving average

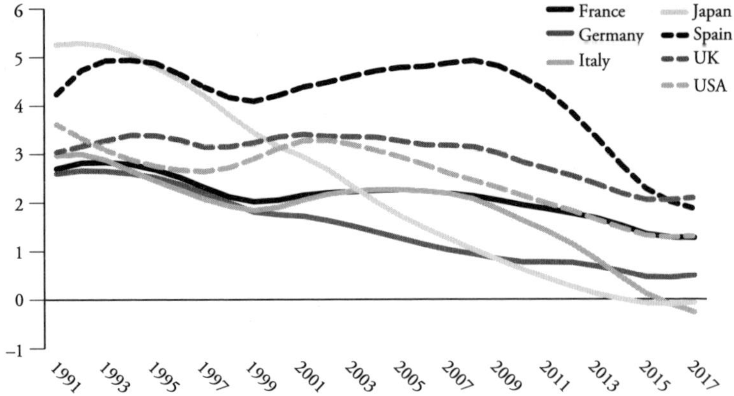

Sources: OECD, TS Lombard, author

capital economies to a limited extent, it also reflects the high rate of write-off in Japan of excessive past capital spending, combined with marginally more modest investment ratios as the country comes to terms with its extremely slow growth.

In Europe, the trends are mixed. Germany, with persistent underestimation of its labour-force growth (and immigration) until recently, has seen capital stock growth slashed to ½% in recent years, a tendency that is likely to be reversed significantly in future. Spain too, having seen its capital stock growth fall to 2% from 4½–5% in the run-up to the crisis, should see a revival now that its competitiveness has been restored by drastic deflation. Italy, on the other hand, is unlikely to reverse the collapse of its real capital stock from over 2% growth into actual decline in recent years. France has seen its capital stock grow much as in the US, while Britain's growth has held up well, and is likely to fall further in future.

But the overall picture is clearly one of declining contribution of real capital input to growth. Some relief from the 'crowding-out'

Figure 9 **Gross world saving, excl. China**
% of GDP

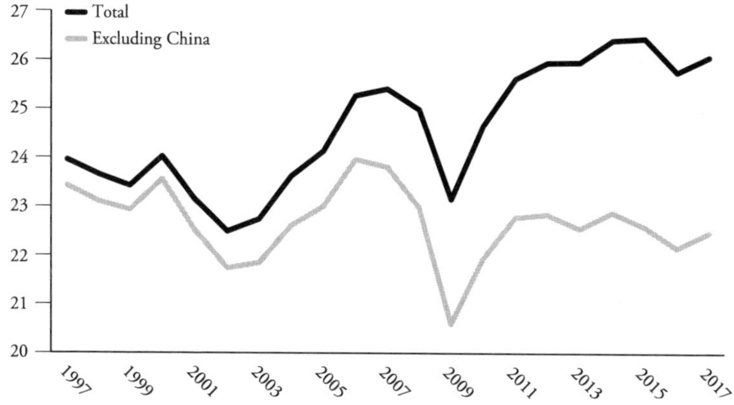

Sources: IMF, CEIC, TS Lombard, author

by excessive Chinese capital spending is likely in future – the likely medium-term rebalancing of China's economy away from excessive capex is described later (Chapter 13). The chart above shows how the *gross* capex ratio for the world excluding China has been on a consistent downward trend since the 1990s. When relatively stable depreciation rates are taken account of, this means the downward trend for net investment – i.e. additions to the net capital stock – has been much sharper.

Some of this downward trend in capex and the capital stock clearly reflects the hysteresis effect of the persistently slow recovery. This is likely to improve only slowly. One likely improvement is less substitution of low-cost labour for capex, as that has been partly driven by fear. 'Post-crisis blues' created uncertainty in business leaders that has induced them to respond to such growth of demand as there has been by taking on extra labour that can be laid off quite quickly in a new crisis, rather than extra capital that will weigh on the balance sheet for a long time. With the sense of never-ending crisis fading, the willingness to commit to extra capital equipment should increase.

The post-crisis blues have a lot to do with the modest growth of wages and consequent lack of inflationary pressure, despite low levels of unemployment in the US, Japan, Germany and Britain. This effect overlaps with the constraint of wages by international competition from low-cost countries – the globalisation effect – and displacement of jobs by hi-tech. But aside from the general caution shown by labour forces globally in the post-crisis environment, the US has seen some reduction of labour mobility.

Labour mobility has always been an important source of resilience of the US economy. But the prevalence of minimal (or even negative) housing equity after the crash for many people, together with banks suddenly insisting on down payments for new mortgage lending in a new location – and probably with house prices higher in a faster-growing region of the country – meant that many people were stuck, unable to consider moving. This severely restricted labour mobility. It also encouraged higher saving, i.e. slower demand.

Additionally, many college graduates suddenly found themselves lumbered with large student debts, discouraging them from striking out even to the extent of taking on a rental contract, let alone home ownership. Outstanding US student debt rose from $400 billion in 2004 to $1.2 trillion in 2014. Now, however, both these negative factors are fading, as house prices rise, and employment amongst the under-30s likewise. The 25–34 age-group now has high employment ratios, and is a growing 'cohort'. It is finally pulling the housing market upward, despite the large baby-boomer cohort tending to downsize in retirement.

Undermining all this concern about a productivity slowdown – particularly for the US economy – is the likelihood that much of the benefit of hi-tech progress is not measured by the estimates of real GDP and its growth. This suspected under-measurement takes four basic forms:

1. Value created that is not properly registered in current-dollar income, output or expenditure
2. Inflation that is overstated, or tech-product deflation that is understated
3. As an extreme form of under-measured inflation, hi-tech value that is free
4. Aspects of hi-tech that generate value with much lesser need for capital input, so that a larger share of total income is available for consumption than previously.

Taking the first and last together, the use of hi-tech for sharing capital resources will tend to lower nominal income (and output and expenditure) while raising real 'income' – the value created in the economy. For example, with Airbnb (house sharing) or Uber (car sharing) the buyer is spending less than for the equivalent service from a hotel or taxi firm. The seller may not declare some – or all – of the income to tax authorities, in which case current-dollar GDP may be significantly reduced. But even if the income is declared GDP will probably be lower, without the buyer suffering loss of value.

While the reduction of current-dollar GDP by the sharing economy may be quite small, the loss of income and usefulness of hotels and taxi firms means their investment in new facilities will be less. This is an example of point (4) above, where the capital needs of the economy are much reduced for a similar level of service output. Fewer cars and accommodations will be needed to serve a given level of demand in the economy. More is therefore available for discretionary consumer income.

The most important example of this capital saving is online shopping. In effect, when I buy through Amazon (for example) my computer stands in for what would otherwise be a shop. My computer has also enabled me to shop around for what I want, and for the best deal, without visiting lots of retail outlets at considerable

Figure 10 **US real gross capex on retail construction, 1956–2016**
2009 = 100

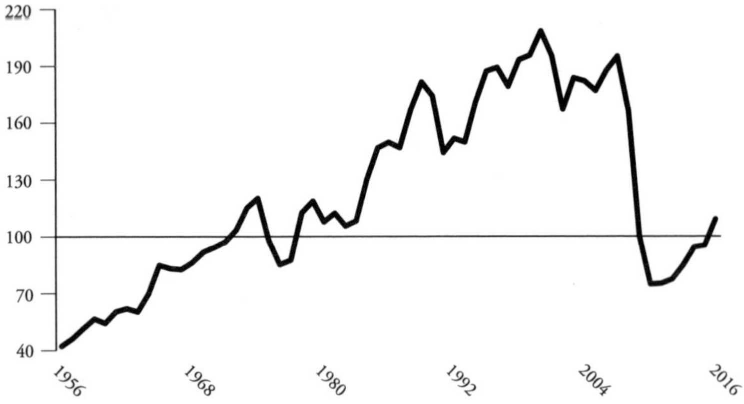

Sources: US BEA, TS Lombard

expense of time and money – an example of item (3) above, free service on the web. The chart above indicates the scale of this saving.

US retail spending on structures – mostly shops – is now about half its end-1990s peak, by when it had risen five times from the mid-1950s. This pressure on former shopping habits is also contributing to downward pressure on retail prices, a further benefit to consumers from hi-tech. The major squeeze on shop-building is partly offset by more warehouses – to permit storage and distribution of items for online shopping.

Google searches are far from the only item effectively free on the web. Much the same is true of email, and even if that leads to unpleasant amounts of junk mail (as does 'snail mail' for that matter), it is a major benefit to people compared with writing letters in the old style. Likewise, in more specialised fashion, with photography. Instead of going out to pay for a camera, and then some film and then, pictures taken, development of the film, people nowadays simply pull out their 'smartphones', which contain cameras that are far better than most in the old days. Large numbers of high-quality photos, including movies, can be shown to friends on computer screens, on the smartphone over lunch, or run off on printers, at minimal expense.

In a more amorphous way, people's use of the web is a form of consumption that is likely to be under-measured. In Britain, for example, the average person spends ten hours a week more on the web now than ten years ago. This could be regarded as the equivalent of three visits to the cinema, essentially free. It is very doubtful if the measures of GDP catch the scale of these free items rising from the web that in the US have been estimated as adding ¼% to annual output growth.

A different form of under-recorded income arises from tax avoidance by large tech monopolies, and other international firms. Patents are lodged in tax havens, and large royalty payments made to them, representing the value of the patent in generating sales. These large royalty payments count as imports, and are a deduction from GDP – and taxable income, of course, reducing tax being the object of the exercise. In the US it is estimated that GDP growth has been cut by another ¼% a year by this means. At the world level, this income should be caught by including the GDP of tax havens, but when people talk of the slowdown of productivity growth they are not generally taking account of its growth in Ireland, say, or the Cayman Islands (assuming, as seems unlikely, it is properly recorded there), to name two important havens.

The second of the four points listed above – overstatement of inflation – is probably the most important single potential understatement of real growth, though it is partly covered by the list of items that are effectively free on the web. Until 2016, studies of the price changes of hi-tech purchases mostly reached the conclusion that the effect of any underestimation has been small. But in 2017, David Byrne at the Fed, one of the chief authors of its 2016 study that vindicated the official data, came up with new estimates suggesting

Figure 11 **Tech-product price deflation**
Official estimates and revised, % change on year earlier

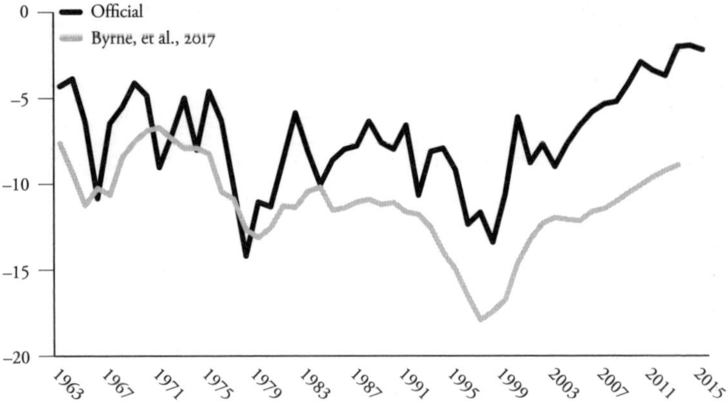

Sources: US BEA, David Byrne, TS Lombard, author

that the price falls in hi-tech products have been far greater than those incorporated in US real GDP estimates (see chart).

If the latest Byrne estimates are correct, with the expenditure covered by the prices in question being more than 6% of GDP, the roughly 6% annual understatement of the price deflation of the past twenty years means the real GDP has been typically growing 0.4% a year faster than officially estimated, while price inflation in the whole economy has been correspondingly overstated.

If this 0.4% is added to the ¼% each already mentioned for the free-services effect and the tax-haven effect, it would add 0.9% to recent annual real US GDP growth. In effect the cyclically adjusted growth rate of productivity would be more than doubled from the officially estimated ¾%, and the real average growth rate since the crisis, instead of the officially measured 2.1%, would be 3%, only a little below the long-run US averages of the second half of the twentieth century.

At a global level this is important, as nobody is surprised, or worried, by the slowdown of China's growth to recent averages of 6½% from the over-10% annual growth achieved in the years to 2011. In India, long-term growth averages are still probably rising, and other developing economies are also growing well, with differences largely representing specific country attributes. So broadening the perspective from the US largely means adding in Europe and Japan. But Japan is a one-off economic malaise to be analysed below (Chapter 12), while Europe has been blighted by the malignant effects of the monetary union – also analysed (Chapter 14), but with the worst of the unnecessary damage probably in the past (though subject to political knock-on effects).

With some modest acceleration of productivity growth likely in future years, the conclusion from this analysis is to focus attention on what clearly has gone wrong – the stagnation of the (real and apparent) standard of living of ordinary people. It is this which has generated the anger expressed in the votes for Brexit – for all the arguments on both sides (see Chapter 15) largely a protest vote – for Trump – with due respect for the social ramifications of America's divisions – and for a plethora of continental European anti-establishment parties, some demagogic, with more likely to come in future. Whatever the benefits to real incomes and people's daily lives from hi-tech and globalisation, it is the real and apparent – perceived – damage to lower-middle-income people that has led to these upheavals.

6

Income distributed away from the lower middle

American commentators often use the phrase 'middle class' to describe middle-to-lower-income people that they wish to refer to without condescension. In Britain the phrase typically refers to a more up-market type of person. 'Lower middle' is used here to duck away from such connotations towards a concept of a broad range of ordinary people, both employed and retired, but excluding those who might be regarded as belonging to an elite or any sort of underclass (or, in a more general sense, 'the poor'). A key point is that in Western society lower-middle people both have the vote and generally use it (unlike the poor).

In twenty-first-century economies the distribution of income has become more equal globally, but less equal in most countries. In advanced countries, whose fortunes still mostly dominate the world economy, the big change has not been a simple increase of inequality between the rich and the poor. The wealth and income increase in the rich versus the lower middle is crucial. Politically, it is proving explosive. Lower-middle voters heavily outweigh the upper echelons of society. The politically motivating issue can be more a matter of perceived unfairness relative to received ideas of what a person is entitled to from society, rather than financial loss as such – though a broad sense of resentment after prolonged income weakness has aggravated things.

Figure 12 **Major countries' GDP and personal disposable income growth**
Per capita, pre- and post-euro, % p.a.

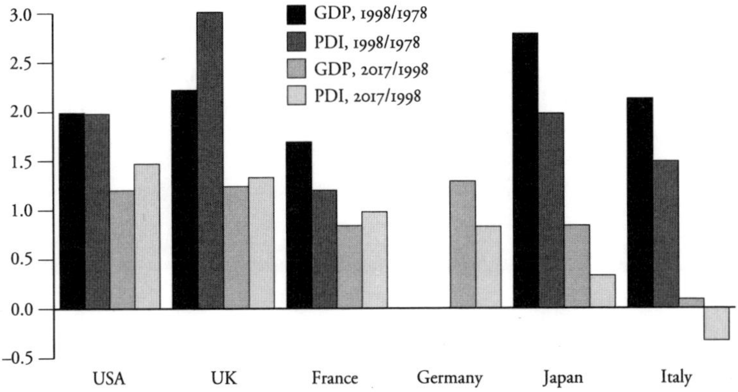

Sources: OECD, TS Lombard, author

The chart above is the starting point for analysis of household income. It shows a clear division between the 'Anglo-Saxons' – the US and UK – and the others. The chart hinges on 1998, as that was the last pre-euro year and also a year in which the world economy was in reasonable balance, though Japan and the Asian Tigers were suffering the worst of the Asian crisis and commodity prices were correspondingly at their low point of the last forty years. The huge surpluses of Japan and the Tigers in response to the crisis (which led to cries of 'never again' and thus a major and determined build-up of reserves) were matched by US deficits, but this imbalance did not seem dangerous in 1998. Growth for all the countries in the chart has been markedly slower post-1998 than before. The worst of this has, of course, been felt since the 2008 financial crisis, and this is probably the chief factor in popular disaffection.

The chart shows the annual change per head of population in both real GDP and real personal disposable (i.e. after-tax) income for the nineteen years from 1998 to 2017, and the twenty years before

1998. (The year 1978 was also middling in cyclical terms, so these numbers are not cyclically distorted.) The distinction between the Anglo-Saxons and the others is that the others were mostly shifting into ever-greater dependence on exports for growth – before the financial crisis in the case of Germany and Japan, and after it for Italy (plus the other stricken 'Club Med' countries). France was an exception, more like the Anglo-Saxons.

The US and UK have achieved reasonable real growth per head in both GDP and disposable household income, around 1¼–1½% a year since 1998, whereas export-dependent countries have seen disposable income fall well behind GDP. France has seen household income match GDP growth, but with significantly slower growth than the US and UK. (Notably, differences of ½% in growth rates over twenty years accumulate to some 10%.) Italy's performance has been particularly disastrous, as real household incomes per head are down over the long term. Italy is the true euro-victim in income terms, Spain in employment terms.

Why did the major political trouble arising from economic weakness happen first in the US and UK? The explanation seems to involve multiple causes:

- Japan's lack of labour militancy is a cultural special case, discussed in Chapter 12.
- Imbalances arising from the euro-system's structure have massively blighted growth on the continent, but at the popular level the euro is not held to blame: it remains popular. Instead, hostility to established elites is growing. Whether the euro-system can (or will) be reformed to cope with imbalances between key nations before populist anger boils over will also be analysed, in Chapter 14.
- The force of populist anger in the US and UK may owe much to the increase of inequality in those two countries, which also have the longest tradition of uninhibited democratic self-expression.

Figure 13 **Gini coefficient of inequality**
%

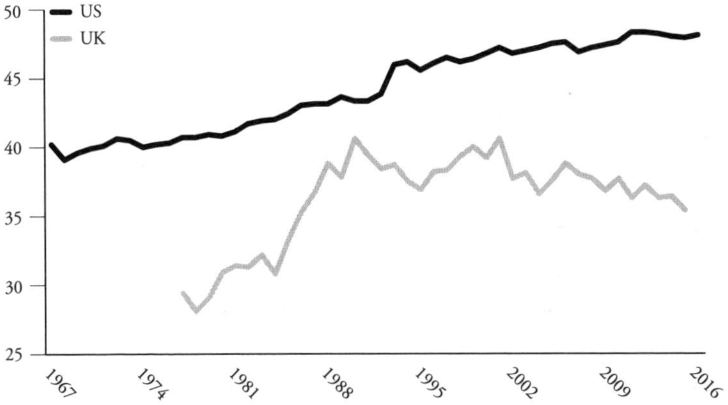

Sources: US Census Bureau, UK National Statistics, TS Lombard, author

The general measure of inequality is the Gini coefficient of inequality, and that has been rising in the US for fifty years, since the late 1960s. The difficulty that this rather dry measure of inequality presents is that there is no intuitive sense of the degree of inequality – let alone inequity – represented by a Gini coefficient of, for example, 40% or 45%. Nor does it discriminate between inequality in which the rich are particularly privileged, as against (for example) the poor being numerous and very much less well off than people on middling incomes.

Also, there is a natural tendency for people to have relatively low incomes in early adulthood, higher incomes later in their working life, and then a lower income in retirement (generally with lower responsibilities). Such inequality is not inequitable, and this generational source of inequality will vary as larger and smaller age cohorts pass through the different stages of their lives. Nonetheless, it is notable that inequality is higher in the US than the UK (and in Europe generally) and still rising. In the UK, after a sharp rise in the 1980s, inequality has fallen slowly, though it remains well above the 1970s level.

Figures 14 and 15 are more concrete illustrations of the emergence of inequality in the US during the years since 2000. The first point to note is that Figure 15 shows how the median US household has had no increase of income since the 2000 peak. The charts all refer to income in constant 2016 dollars, i.e. real income at recently current prices. The 2007 peak was just below the 2000 and 2016 level. The median income is the level with exactly half the population getting more and half getting less. This is the best measure of where the 'average person' lies. The 'mean' income is the average for the population, which gives greater weight to high and ultra-high incomes: in Figure 14 it is used to show the gain in average real income for the different portions of the overall income distribution.

The fact that median household income has not gone up this century is in sharp contrast with the nearly 1½% annual increase shown overleaf in real average US personal disposable since 1998 – the growth rate since 2000 being only a little less at 1.3%. Compounded over sixteen years, this is an increase of 24%. Clearly, the data in the charts opposite, sourced from the US Census department, are not directly comparable with the real personal income numbers adjusted for population growth. In particular, the average size of households must have been falling to create the discrepancy. Nonetheless, these charts are entirely relevant to discussion of the distribution of income, as between income quintiles and different educational backgrounds.

Stagnation of median household real income is itself frustrating, compared with twentieth-century experience. As average income has gone up a lot, the increases have been concentrated amongst those already on higher incomes. Figure 14 illustrates this effect clearly. The experience of the middle (i.e. the third) fifth – virtually no change between 2000 and 2016 – corresponds to the unchanged

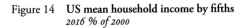

Figure 14 **US mean household income by fifths**
2016 % of 2000

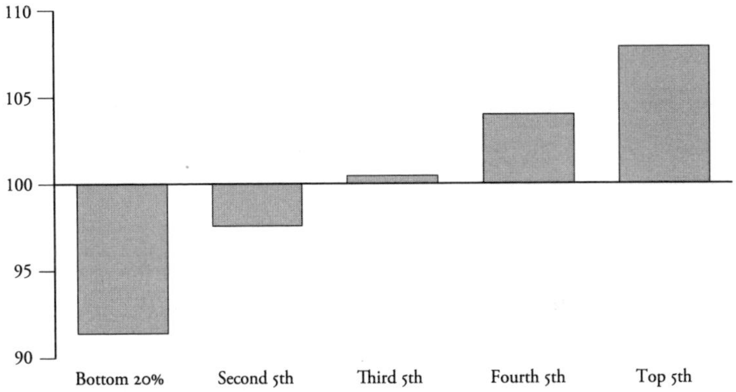

Sources: US Census Bureau, TS Lombard, author

Figure 15 **US median household income by educational attainment**
2016 % of 2000

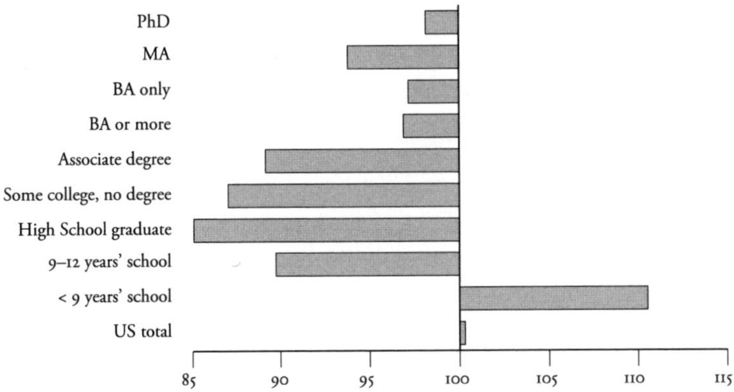

Sources: US Census Bureau, TS Lombard, author

median for the whole population. The poorer two-fifths did worse and the richer two-fifths better, in a very straightforward progression. It is not difficult to see why the bottom three-fifths of the income distribution could feel angry.

The Figure 15 analysis of the shift since 2000 of median incomes by educational attainment would appear to be biased downward in its statistical sources, as all groups appear worse off except the least educated – which must be quite a small group, given the worse results for the bottom one-fifth shown in Figure 14. But while Figure 15 may be biased in its basic sources, it clearly points to worse experience this century for lower-middle people – those with only high school education, or a smattering of college but no BA.

It is good to look at the relevant facts, but voting stems to a great degree from perceptions. These may differ from reality, but how they are formed still matters. In the case of inequality people may have their views based on daily life – other people they rub up against at work, as they commute to work, in shops, the pub, whatever. But the prevalence of social media in modern society makes impressions of how celebrities and the rich are living a more present reality than in the past. The bulk of those people – 'celebrities' – viewed vicariously in this way fall in the 'top 1%' of income recipients.

Ordinary people's consciousness and potential resentment of inequality is affected by their view of the relative position of the 'top 1%'. Also, resentment in the post-crisis West reflects perceptions of inequitable sharing of the 'pain' of the crisis. In this respect, the chief difference is more trans-Atlantic than between the US–UK and continental Europeans. A generally rising incomes share for the top 1% from the 1970s into the first decade of this century has reversed a little in Germany, France and the UK. But the distribution of income in the USA, already more unequal, has got more so. This is even more true of the top 1%'s wealth.

These data suggest some degree of commonality in the West, as

Figure 16 **Top 1%: income**
%

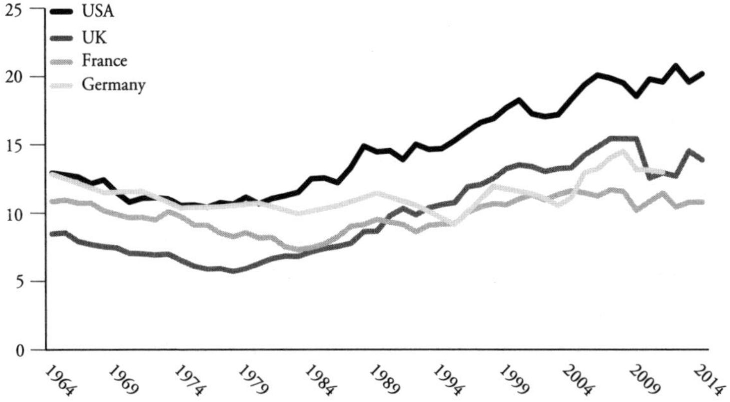

Sources: World Inequality Database, TS Lombard, author

Figure 17 **Top 1%: wealth**
%

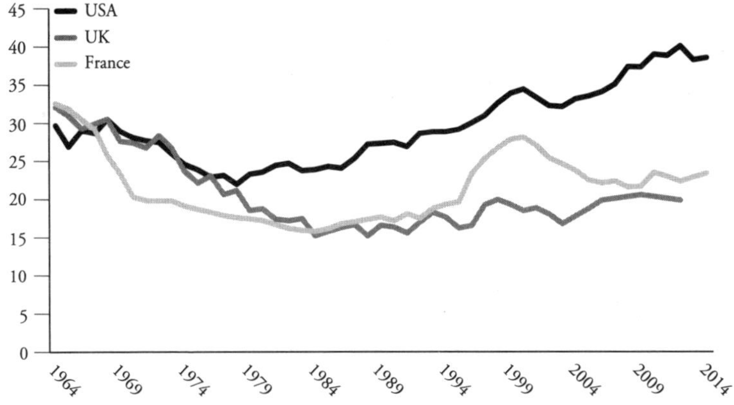

Sources: World Inequality Database, TS Lombard, author

would be expected given the common experience of globalisation and hi-tech applications. Also in common has been the emphasis on monetary policy as a cure for sluggish growth. With such 'secular stagnation' as there has been largely caused by structural, non-monetary factors – and different from country to country, both globally and within the EA – monetary policy has often been ineffective. As it also involves QE practically everywhere, and both QE and lower interest rates are expected to stimulate the economy primarily by the indirect means of raising wealth to generate spending, the combination of great wealth, naturally concentrated in the rich, and lack of adequate impact on growth has aggravated social tensions in most of the West. (QE is analysed in Chapters 7–10.)

But the differences between countries are also clear. The Trump vote has to be viewed in the context of a continued rapid increase in the US of both wealth and income inequality. Aggravating this, the negligible growth of median family income is both long-lasting – i.e. from 2000, not just the crisis – and has to be set against the use of government powers to 'protect Wall Street, but not Main Street': a major contribution to the increase of inequality this century. In continental Europe, the chief pain has arisen from the general economic failures caused by euro-related imbalances. In Britain, the linguistic and cultural links to the USA may mean some of the attitude that caused the Brexit vote reflected US rather than British conditions, but it is doubtful if inequality – rather than a variety of other factors – was decisive (see Chapter 15).

Scarcely relevant to all this was the analysis of Thomas Piketty in his *Capital in the Twenty-First Century*. His book gave an algebraic demonstration of why he thought inequality is likely to increase. But his concern about the combination of slower growth and heritability of wealth does not fit what has happened since 1980. The chief source of increasing inequality has been the globalisation, technology, US tax changes to benefit the rich, and other effects already described, not inheritance. And his algebra is far from conclusive as regards the long-term future. But he and others, including Gabriel Zucman, who has written a useful book about tax havens, are developing valuable statistics on inequality that yielded the 1% share data above. The current situation and immediate developments are explosive enough, without Piketty's projection of a further century of increased inequality!

While the erosion of real labour incomes in advanced countries by globalisation may become less severe in future, as countries like China catch up and diversify away from low-end manufacturing, the impact of hi-tech could intensify. Plants that are fully automatic and only require maintenance engineers are already common, and the much-ballyhooed advent of driverless vehicles could also cost a lot of jobs. Higher up the income scale, large swathes of lawyering could be automated – to take an example of a profession that has been effective in preserving non-tariff barriers to globalisation (as well as much else).

Clearly, the pace of change is the key factor here, not the fact of it – without some such progress, rising real incomes would become history. And if my car was as reliable as my computer, I would refuse to drive it, so driverless vehicles may come in a lot more slowly than some futurists imagine. But major transformation of the way we live and work is liable to mean a lot of people get 'left on the shelf'. So hi-tech causes of neo-Luddite attitudes may increase rather than soften over the next decade or two. Empathy with the losers from technical progress will remain essential for the foreseeable future.

Tax policy and fiscal policy issues generally are an important part of the argument about inequality. The steeper gains in the 1% share of income in the US and UK compared to France and Germany are partly owing to tax changes. The Bush Junior US administration cut taxes on incomes generally, but most of all for high incomes, as almost its first act on attaining power in 2001. Economically, its stance was justified by the economy flirting with recession after the bursting of the stock market tech bubble in 2000. But taxes on the rich were then further heftily cut in 2003. In Britain the largest upswing of inequality as measured by the Gini coefficient was in the 1980s, when the Thatcherite programme involved a significant shift in the burden of taxes onto spending, with lower income tax, especially the top rates (which in the 1970s had been raised as high as 98%). This inevitably contributed to the increase of inequality. But inequality of wealth has increased significantly since the late 1980s.

We have already noticed (p. 8) that a feature of the savings glut in both the West and Pacific Rim countries has been increased emphasis on business saving – depreciation and retained profits. In the Pacific Rim this tendency seems more cultural than tax-driven, and its stultifying effects will be analysed below in chapters on China, and on Japan and Korea as well as in Appendix 2.

But in the West the increase of business saving has been at least partly the result of tax avoidance, and has therefore been fiscally damaging as well as a source of financial imbalances. Together with tax avoidance by individuals – also often involving use of tax havens – this has not only added to inequality, but also to the perception of policy favouring 'Wall Street over Main Street' that is threatening the genuine worldwide income and welfare benefits of globalisation and technology. Clearly, tax avoidance, leaving aside its offensive aspect, requires either higher taxes on middle incomes, or greater austerity in government spending programmes – a double whammy in terms of 'reverse Robin Hood' transfers from poor to rich.

As reliance on monetary solutions to economic problems has also aggravated inequality, the whole question of the fiscal/monetary policy balance, together with other relevant policy issues affecting growth and welfare, requires analysis, before we examine the individual countries and regions. Tax issues are examined as an appendix to the chapter on conclusions and recommendations.

7

Keynes vs Friedman, the bogus dilemma

Apologies to Sir Samuel Brittan, who fifty years ago wrote a book entitled *Left Or Right: The Bogus Dilemma*. John Maynard Keynes and Milton Friedman are two of the most brilliant economists ever – arguably, two of the most brilliant *people* ever. It is extraordinary that apparently high-powered enthusiasts for the one or the other have expended so much intellectual and emotional energy bad-mouthing the unfavoured one.

Historically, governments were judged incapable of affecting the economic cycle. At best they should concentrate on improving supply-side conditions with (for instance) broad-based, low and equitable taxes, and avoidance of corruption, waste and (ideally) war. Such was the view of Adam Smith in his 1776 *Wealth of Nations*, which can only be properly understood in the ethical context of his *The Theory of Moral Sentiments* (1759). The pursuit of his policies by William Pitt the Younger, UK prime minister from 1783, despite his inability to avoid prolonged war with France, helped the historic breakthrough embodied in the Industrial Revolution – even if that did have its dark side that gave birth to Luddism ('dark, satanic mills', etc.).

In the nineteenth century the dominant economic attitudes were developed by David Ricardo and Alfred Marshall, applying imaginative thought and mathematical rigour to supply-side views, particularly the benefits of free trade. The regulation of the economic cycle – i.e. the demand side – remained the role of the banking system and the level of interest rates. It was not regarded as offering scope for public policy as such. Walter Bagehot, in his 1873 *Lombard Street: A Description of the Money Market*, described how a central bank should handle a panic, but firefighting is not the same as preventing fires. Growth and spreading of the wealth was extremely impressive over the long run, but punctuated with vicious downswings.

Unregulated capitalism developed other enemies than the revolutionary proponents of Marxism, for example the populist William Jennings Bryan in the 1890s US, who excoriated the 'cross of gold' – gold supply providing an artificial and largely arbitrary base to the crucially important money supply. Despite losing three runs for president (in 1896, 1900 and 1908), the idea of a government role in stabilising the economic cycle gained credence after the Gilded Era, in which inequality increased enormously, still with plenty of financial crises. The 'Panic of 1893' and the 'Panic of 1906' (the 'Rich Man's Panic', eventually ended by the intervention of J. P. Morgan) reinforced disillusion with the gold standard. The US Federal Reserve system was established in 1913, with the hope that it would avoid repetition of such crises by regulating the money supply.

Some hope! After the 'Roaring Twenties' – which did not roar very loud in a Europe devastated by the First World War – the US collapsed into the 1930s Great Depression. Keynes, already as masterly a monetary economist as any, identified two 'structural' weaknesses of the economic system that made the classical reliance on variations of interest rates and on quantitative control of the money supply insufficient to prevent depressions. A social/political structural obstacle was the downside 'stickiness' of wages. In everyday English, people strongly and violently oppose accepting a pay cut. More generally and largely since Keynes's day, behavioural economic theory has taught us that people's feelings about gains and losses are not symmetrical. People are typically much more upset by a loss than they are pleased by an equivalent gain.

The second rigidity that Keynes identified as preventing the cure for a depression is the 'zero lower bound' for interest rates. While lower interest rates were supposed in classical theory to regenerate investors' 'animal spirits', bringing economic downswings to an end, Keynes conceived that the interest rate at which such a transition would be effected might be well below zero. In that case lenders would simply tend to hold on to the cash rather than accept the built-in loss of a negative interest rate loan. This is the famous 'liquidity trap'.

The Great Depression's deep deficiency of spending that Keynes saw as insoluble within the classical framework could, of course, knock on to a prolonged weakness that would undermine the supply side – most obviously by a shortage of capital investment, but also, for example, by a deterioration of skills and energy in the labour force, with a large direct human cost. So his solution, 'Keynesianism', was for the government to offset the shortage of private demand with 'negative saving': spending more than its revenue to make up the deficiency. This could take the form either of spending increases or tax cuts – with varying consequences. But the concept was the same: the government would cure a depression by direct demand stimulus funded by debt.

Keynesian theory was relatively triumphant intellectually by the 1950s, even if his remedies had only been partially applied, and that mostly in the US by the Roosevelt administration. Keynes's remedies were in effect also adopted by Hitler in rearming Germany, and the Second World War in general cured the deficiency of demand – a sad case of the cure being worse than the disease. But the deep scars of depression and war – with the former widely held to have caused the latter – left post-war ruling establishments determined to avoid any risk of a repeat.

World War II had been to a great degree won by the Communist

Soviet Union, at least in Europe. Western elites were on the defensive. The genuine Keynesian idea of using budget deficits to cure depressions morphed into using the budget balance to regulate and smooth the economic cycle. This was quickly conflated with the assumption by governments of much greater participation in the economy, not merely to provide traditional 'public goods' – defence, education, roads, etc. – but also ownership of many less obviously suitable industries, such as telecoms, water supply and energy utilities. This paralleled a general acceptance of government responsibility for fast growth, low unemployment and redistribution to achieve general prosperity.

Circumstances were favourable, and US policies to pump-prime the rebuilding of Europe and Japan were admirable: a fine show of enlightened self-interest. The rigours of depression and war had left a huge pent-up demand for goods and services, reinforced by lively growth of birth rates and populations. Governments lurched into deficit financing at the first sign of any slackening in the hectic pace of advance. As a result, labour forces gradually lost any sense of the risk in pursuit of higher incomes. Fuelled by the US pursuit of the 'Great Society' at the same time as waging the Vietnam War – so-called 'guns and butter' – inflation took off. Restraint in demands for higher wages that had prevailed through the 1950s gave way to the ethos of prolonged and apparently invincible prosperity.

Inflation lowered the 'real' price of oil – though it was nominally unchanged for years – just as the general worldwide boom and the specifics of the Vietnam War increased the demand for it. This imbalance was resolved drastically when the Arab members of OPEC took the opportunity of the Yom Kippur War in September 1973 first to boycott oil exports to the US (as military supplier to Israel) and then to raise crude oil prices fourfold. The resultant jump of general inflation combined with reduced real incomes in practically all advanced economies (being net importers of oil) led to a crisis and recession comparable to the later 'great recession' of 2009.

What to do about simultaneously rocketing inflation and

unemployment? Should you restrain the economy to curb inflation, or stimulate it to reduce unemployment? So-called Keynesians, still remembering the 1930s, favoured fiscal stimulus, but were genuinely confused. A deeper understanding of Keynesian thinking could have led to a more laissez-faire view. The needed reduction of real incomes, particularly wages, arising from the higher real cost of oil and other commodities, would not require nominal wage cuts – the bête noire of Keynes. Merely holding wages steady would lower their real buying power, owing to inflation. The contrast was clear between Germany, which more or less implemented this principle, and Britain, where 1974's new Minister of Labour, Michael Foot, declared at a time of inflation approaching 25% that wage increases of 30% were 'well within the terms of the social contract'. Germany came out of the first oil crisis relatively well; 1970s Britain was the economic cripple of the advanced world.

The point goes beyond just wage rigidity. Just as real wages could be adjusted downward without nominal cuts – the *casus belli* of the 1926 UK General Strike – so could real interest rates be reduced well below zero by inflation even if nominal rates remained positive. Getting below the 'zero bound' was not difficult in the mid-1970s. So the advocates of monetary restraint had the upper hand in the argument with so-called Keynesians (amongst whom it is doubtful if Keynes himself would have been numbered).

Monetary restraint was in any case clearly likely to be effective against inflation, but just as soon as the economy fell back so would nominal interest rates. With inflation only coming down gradually, real interest rates would become negative and – especially as asset prices nose-dived to attractive levels – investors' animal spirits would revive.

Of course the real world is a muddle, and commodity price cycles are violent, often self-feeding. It took another round of the same process to effect the full transition from cod-Keynesian to monetarist dominance, with Paul Volcker, as chairman of the Fed, shaking down the world economy in 1980–82. As the whole process involved the acceptance of limits, in this case imposed by oil prices, but implicitly dooming the entire hubristic edifice of 'guns and butter' thinking that prevailed in the late 1960s, it was also in essence conservative.

What was less 'conservative' (small 'c') was radical reversal of the mission creep from Keynesian attitudes about unemployment to virtually unlimited enlargement of the role of the state. Just as fiscal remedies for the oil crises were rightly rejected, monetarists re-emphasised the benefits of free markets and private enterprise, reverting to Adam Smith's principles (though he in his day had been what might now be called leftist or even populist). These ideas, more prevalent in the US and UK than continental Europe and Japan, were vindicated by much better Anglo-Saxon countries' growth from 1980 onward (as the chart on p. 59 above makes clear).

The lessons for the current situation are clear, and point away from the monetarist consensus of the past forty years. The 1930s crisis featured chronically weak demand. The 1970s crisis featured chronically excessive demand. The first required a fiscal cure, the second a monetary cure – in both cases contrary to initial establishment thinking, the previously 'received wisdom'. The savings glut as the source of the 2007–9 financial crisis and great recession, as well as a major factor in the weak recovery from it, is a case of chronically weak demand. Yet fiscal measures were only briefly applied in 2009–10, after which the burden of supporting recovery fell almost entirely on the monetary authorities.

Nearly ten years after the financial crisis and great recession, much of the argument for fiscal stimulus – Keynesian deficits – is weakened by the passage of time, and the adjustments already made in the most damaged economies, e.g. Spain, to the policies actually adopted. There remains a substantial measure of international payments imbalances, now largely concentrated in continental Europe, but the cure for that lies in real exchange rate changes more than fiscal policies – though some fiscal stimulus may well be tried.

What emerges from all this is that the pursuit of monetarist stimulus as the chief means of dealing with inadequate demand has been a mistake. A variety of structural changes need to be adopted to deal with different countries' problems, to counter the genesis and aggravation of the crucial problem of stagnant to falling living standards amongst ordinary working people.

8

The failure of monetarist solutions

Little of the relatively upbeat analysis here of current and prospective growth owes anything to the chief economic policy instrument in use globally: monetary action. Hi-tech progress is purely a supply-side story. Globalisation may optimise the world's welfare, and generally does so even for advanced countries considered alone, but it imposes wrenching adjustments on ordinary people. The theories that seemed to be proved right for the anti-inflationary requirements of the 1980s and 1990s have proved weak in combatting both debt crisis and its aftermath, and are irrelevant to coping with problems arising from globalisation and the hi-tech transformation of the supply side.

The world has seen since the financial crisis and great recession

- failure to pursue the '3 Ds' solution to debt crises in continental Europe
- refusal of Germany and failure by Japan to accept responsibility for acting as global locomotives for the world economy
- more general hostility to sustained fiscal stimulus, owing to the memory of dire 1970s inflation.

All that was left was the 1980s monetarist/liberal-supply-side mantra. That monetary effects are not symmetrical led to the 1930s metaphor about pushing on a piece of string. Restrictive monetary policy to curb inflation is pulling on a piece of string. It worked well to that effect from 1979–80 onward under the leadership of the Fed's Paul Volcker. But monetary stimulus to generate economic recovery from a slump is like pushing on a piece of string. What makes this worse is that in current conditions it necessarily sharply increases inequality of wealth – often benefiting exactly the people who were directly responsible for the financial crisis.

To be fair to the Fed and the Bank of England, the monetary stimulus they adopted – quantitative easing, QE – did help to achieve their immediate goal: to stave off any repetition of the 1930s catastrophe. But in combination with other measures adopted and not adopted by the chief authorities concerned, as well as the disastrous conduct of policy in the euro area, the focus of recovery policies on monetary measures alone has been deeply suboptimal:

- Bank rescues, without adequate punishment of the bankers whose bad loans had caused the crisis, left in place the majority of the blameworthy people in jobs where high incomes were quickly restored – in contrast to the rest of the economy.
- Failure to adopt badly needed debt write-offs outside the US, and the devaluations of debtor-country currencies, reinforced the privileging of banks at the expense of the rest of the population, and preserved the savings glut that underlies global imbalances.
- The successful and badly needed US dollar devaluation of 2010–12, a major benefit flowing from the US Fed's QE, was progressively undone by beggar-my-neighbour devaluations, under the pretext of QE-based monetary easing in Japan (in early 2013 and again from mid-2014) and the EA from mid-2014.
- The ECB's scrabbling for the devaluation desperately needed by Italy and Greece – and to a lesser extent Spain, Portugal and Ireland – also massively lowered the real exchange rate of Germany and surrounding countries, reinforcing global imbalances.

- Japan adopted Abenomics, trying to achieve growth and inflation by devaluation and export stimulus, but by that very means increased Japan's crucial domestic income imbalance – much too much bottled-up business income and much too little household income. Devaluation switches income into profits (i.e. business) and away from labour (i.e. households).
- The EA, diverted into the irrelevant, revived 'Stability and Growth Pact', sought balanced budgets as a priority over all else. Fiscal tightening in already over-competitive German-centred Europe added to the imbalances and surpluses caused by massive demand deflation in Mediterranean Europe and, from mid-2014, the ECB's devaluation policy to rescue it.
- The damage to Britain from the EA's domestic demand weakness, appreciation of the pound as the euro foundered, and migration of labour from stricken Mediterranean Europe was decisive in shifting opinion in favour of Brexit at an inopportune time, and without any preparation – though the ambitions of the EA to form a unified economy, if successful (which is open to severe doubts), would probably have led to *de facto* Brexit, or some other form of exclusion of EA non-members in due course.

This grim list of specific policy deficiencies will be fully analysed in the sections below on the various countries. But as well as this, the attempt at stimulus by monetary means alone is objectionable in principle. Most obviously, the mechanism of monetary stimulus depends heavily on the wealth effect: by raising the value of real assets – real property, and stocks and shares – monetary stimulus supposedly induces people to invest to create more such assets 'at cost price'. The extra money created and passed on in this way then supposedly burns a hole in people's pockets, increasing spending.

All of this can happen, and to a (regrettably inadequate) degree has happened – but what happened first was that the kind of people who own real assets in the first place got much better off: inequality was increased. Monetary stimulus as the nearly exclusive policy for recovery reinforced the schism between 'elites' and ordinary people that arose from prioritising rescue for the banks over more general schemes for broad-based economic recovery.

9

The folly of inflation targets

A further objection to the focus on monetary methods of stimulus is that it is embodied in a peculiar, perverse goal: *raising* inflation to reach a given target. For most of the advanced countries, 2% inflation is the target. It is one thing to adopt an inflation target when inflation is rampant and needs to be reduced: the existence of the target can help formulation and acceptance of the necessary steps. But it is absurd to try to create inflation when there is none.

In Japan, price deflation had been normal by early in the recovery for not far short of twenty years. And the country had a large overseas surplus, implying a strong currency that should further deflate prices. The fact that Japan's post-2012 policy was to devalue is a good illustration of the perversity of a positive inflation target. This devaluation increased financial imbalances both domestically and globally. In the EA fears of deflation were rife even before the oil-price crash brought actual price falls, despite coincident euro devaluation. And the huge EA overseas surplus almost certainly presages a major rise in the euro that will hold inflation down after its modest revival of the past couple of years.

Interestingly, even US inflation is arguably close to zero. The 'core' rate (CPI excluding food and energy) is 1½–2% to be sure, but exclusion of housing rents cuts this to less than 1%. The rapid inflation of rents largely reflects shortage of house-building in the long, deep slump from 2007 until 2012 – set against a 25–34-year-old generation that is now growing significantly after previous declines (around the turn of the century) and is also back to full employment. In the general market economy the going rate of inflation is thus only 1%. And the under-measurement of tech effects referred to above (p. 53) suggests that the 'true' number could be only about half that. For practical purposes, the US has little or no inflation.

If the natural rate of inflation in current conditions in the US, continental Europe and Japan is at or close to zero, why should one wish to raise it to 2%? Apologists mutter about inflation being needed to achieve a hidden debt write-off – as if anybody still suffers from the 'money illusion' and is easily deceived about the effects of inflation on interest-bearing investments. The truth is that the 2% number is entirely arbitrary. But the active determination to create inflation out of thin air is open to both theoretical and extremely practical objections.

One theoretical snag is that money is supposed to fulfil three functions, and the economy is damaged if it does not. The three functions are to be a means of exchange, a unit of account and a store of value. With inflation, money's function as a store of value is obviously reduced, if not wiped out. As a unit of account it is also weakened, as evidenced by the adjustments that analysts of company accounts had to make – very often unsuccessfully – to deal with the distortions of values resulting from inflation in the 1970s.

10

Inflation targets threaten boom–bust

At a more practical level, pursuit of 2% inflation, when the natural rate is close to zero, threatens boom–bust – a stock market bubble followed by a sharp bear market. Whatever the specific means by which inflation is induced to accelerate, it clearly involves overheating the economy. An overheated economy is one that is growing substantially faster than its potential rate, with falling unemployment reaching levels that stoke up wage and price inflation. If inflation is raised to 2% by this means, it will necessarily go through 2% on the upside.

It is not possibly to swing an economy overnight from overheated back below its potential level, enabling slack in the economy to bring inflation back under control. Restrictive policies as the inflation rate climbs above 2%, and the normal lags of economies in response to policies of eighteen months or so, make a reversal into an economic downswing (at best, a slump at worst) almost inevitable.

Financial markets will tend to lead this process with bubble and then bust – they are the means by which monetary policy has its effects. The process is already under way. The US Fed is the central bank most advanced in withdrawing stimulus. Its QE stopped from 2014 onward and is partially reversed now ('quantitative tightening', or QT), with several interest-rate hikes since the post-recession lows. Yet US short-term rates are still below inflation – negative in 'real' terms. The long-run average for US short-term interest rates is inflation plus 2%, and that includes recession periods as well as booms. The Fed's estimate of the 'neutral' real rate now is ¾%. Yet the rate is negative still in actuality.

US monetary policy thus remains clearly stimulative. Yet the economy has been growing faster than its potential by some ½–¾% a year for nine years now, since mid-2009, with unemployment falling rapidly to around the lowest levels since the late 1960s – and highly likely to fall further. To be applying monetary stimulus in such an environment – especially after the passage of fiscal stimulus in the form of a tax cut – is inviting trouble. Profits could boom and the mountain of unspent liquidity from years of monetary ease is likely to crash into financial markets causing them to 'melt up' … and then in traditional stop-go style – or go-stop in this case – policy will be tightened: too much, too late.

If US policy looks wrong, the EA's is worse, only mitigated by the impossibility of devising a 'right' monetary policy for a currency that includes Germany and Italy, whose needs are only too obviously radically different. The current policy ensures ongoing QE right through September 2018, if at half the rate of 5% of GDP that prevailed in 2017. Meanwhile short-term interest rates are significantly negative even in nominal terms, and far below the core inflation rate of 1¼%. Yet the EA has enjoyed above-potential growth for five years, and inflation, though still below target, has risen despite euro appreciation.

The only plausible motivation for this astonishingly excessive stimulus is protection of the extremely weak recovery in Italy. Italy's real output remains a grim 5–6% below its pre-crisis peak of ten years ago. The inflation target of 2% is largely a fig leaf masking this Italian-support policy.

To be fair, the EA economy has removed slack, and is only modestly above-potential in level after the euro crisis of 2010–13 ensured a six-quarter double-dip recession to early 2013. It is not yet seriously overheated. But its growth is above-potential, and unemployment is coming down quite fast. The huge overseas surplus means that the euro will probably appreciate substantially in future, tending to hold down the inflation rate. This could be used to justify monetary stimulus way beyond the end of 2018. Yet the overall condition of the EA economy suggests policy should be broadly neutral – which might mean short-term rates of 2% and no QE, rather than -0.4% and substantial QE. This will be truer still if, as is likely, Italy, Germany and (maybe) France soon engage in some fiscal stimulus.

As it is, monetary policy is injecting powerful stimulus in the US, throughout Europe and in Japan, where interest rates are locked in below zero and QE is running at 6% of GDP, having been 2½–3 times that from 2013 to 2016. Some argue that this has already provoked a bubble, with stocks much overvalued. My analysis suggests only modest overvaluation so far, the bubble danger being still in the future. If that develops, it would in due course force a reaction into heavily restrictive policies, provoking a downswing that the relatively strong state of the world economy makes entirely unnecessary. And this downswing will be 'owned' by the central banks and the policy elite.

Few people forecast the financial crisis ten years ago, though this author was one of them. Being surprised by it was a respectable position. A policy paradigm did not emerge to replace the 'monetarism with a liberal supply side' that served the world well from 1979–80 to the end of the twentieth century. The former medicine was applied without significant amendment to the reverse situation, demand followed by price deflation, for which it was inappropriate. There is no symmetry between inflation and deflation. And this outdated policy paradigm enabled politicians and their advisers to hide behind the monetarist consensus, rather than think through the requirement of the new problems from first principles.

Widespread contempt for elites has regrettably strong justification. The revolt of working Westerners against the stagnation of incomes, disrespect for their ideas of fairness and seeming failure of the economic policy paradigm has every chance of growing more intense, as hi-tech chisels away at livelihoods, and wealth becomes more unequal. The risk is that a decade of serious disappointment blows out into an unnecessary boom–bust, and relapse into stop–go, with dangerous political consequences.

11

Tax distortions and avoidance worsen the savings glut

One aspect of recent 'liberal' world economic conditions that encourages contempt for elites is that when it comes to paying taxes there seems to be one rule for the rich and a stricter one for everyone else. Elaborate tax-avoidance schemes – as opposed to taking intended advantage of specific incentives – are expensive. Only if large amounts of income get 'protected' from high rates of taxes does the expense make sense.

Similarly with corporate taxation, only companies operating internationally can take advantage of a choice of venues for location of headquarters, and/or valuable assets such as key patents, to which profits can be directed. This undermines their single-country competitors that are unable to dodge tax with these artificial devices. Yet single-country firms create and sustain the majority of jobs – and quite possibly of innovation too, at least at the early stage.

The broad forms of personal tax avoidance, generally involving the use of tax havens, clearly damage economies. The post-crisis period has seen much of the private debt that led to crisis in the US, Club Med (especially Spain and Portugal) and Britain and Ireland shifted to government balance sheets. This has been partly because of fiscal deficits in the early recovery period to pull economies out of recession, and partly through restructuring of private debts and of bad banks sponsored and generally underwritten by governments.

Without the loss of revenue to tax avoidance, governments could either have had less of a debt build-up, or could have provided more fiscal stimulus via spending or tax cuts.

To be sure, cash built up in private accounts, whether or not in tax havens, will have been put to work in investments in substantive economies. But for the most part this would not have taken the form of direct spending, but rather purchases of existing assets. In this it is most akin in its benefits to QE, or monetary stimulus in general. But such investment fits well the metaphor of 'pushing on a piece of string' that has weakened the impact of monetary stimulus. And in an even more obvious way than QE it operates by increasing inequality – in this case with enrichment that is directly contrary to the intentions of government tax policies.

Governments have not been keen, however, to turn away such cash inflows. First, tax-dodge-funded inflows to any one country are for the most part at the expense of another country's tax revenues; in any case the revenue loss is 'water under the bridge'. Second, such inflows, while less beneficial than direct investment spending, bring some benefits, and also are important income sources for influential lobbies such as lawyers and accountants, even if the activities financed by the inflows are of at best marginal economic benefit. And when the head of a small country conspicuous mostly for sponsoring tax avoidance can leverage that job to become President of the European Commission, the cost/benefit balance in being a tax haven is clearly wrong.

Corporate tax avoidance through such devices as the location of patents in tax-haven countries aggravates the effects of the savings glut. At the level of national income, a portion of what should be domestic income is siphoned away as service imports to the haven's income. For the US, this effect is estimated to have reduced national output and income growth by ¼% a year in recent years, $50 billion a year. As the build-up is estimated to have reached $3 trillion stored away in haven countries, notably not just in such as the Caribbean and the Channel Islands but also Ireland, Holland and Luxembourg, this $50 billion deduction from annual growth could well be an underestimate.

To the extent US firms are spending the cash kept abroad for dividends or capital spending, it adds to US corporate debt, as the overseas cash has to be replicated via onshore borrowing. Alarm calls have been heard about corporate debt levels relative to income. At this point these calls seem premature, though some upward pressure on interest rates has to have resulted. But if the economy really gets going, as seems to be starting to happen, and interest rates go up significantly, these business debt levels may start to be a concern, and an inhibition on the economy.

Loss of income through tax avoidance (or evasion) raises a country's balance of payments deficit. This has to be financed. It is through debt build-ups of this kind that the savings glut caused the financial crisis in 2007–9 – in that instance the US culprit was housing debt, particularly sub-prime. Likewise it is the need to control such debt build-ups that has provoked the private-sector debt deflation and government austerity programmes of the years since 2009, including the euro crisis. Estimates of the assets held outside Greece by its citizens, for example, exceed the country's public-sector debt. Few doubt that a major portion of such assets have been built up abroad precisely in order to avoid tax.

Measures to reduce or eliminate tax avoidance by individuals are outside the scope of this book, but a general point can be made: taxes on the rich in the form of property, land or wealth taxes are economically preferable to taxes on high incomes. This applies to company taxation too. Where assets are used effectively, income will be higher. Waste will be penalised, as loss of income will not lower the tax due on assets used. Income taxes are a disincentive to effective use of assets. Taxes on assets, no matter how much income they generate, are preferable not just because they avoid such disincentives, but also because they penalise people that keep assets idle or unproductive. Appendix 1 to this book on taxation examines this more closely.

12

Japan – fertile ground for populist revolt

Tax avoidance and cash bottled up abroad may be causing significant damage to the advanced economies and social cohesion in North America and Europe. But in Japan the build-up of corporate cash is the *primary* source of the economy's failures, both on the demand side and the supply side. This has been extremely costly for Japanese citizens. Why, it must be asked, is there not the same anti-establishment revulsion there as in the West? Currently healthy worldwide growth is providing Japan with the export-led growth that is the only mode it has proved capable of. But the analysis to be presented here suggests that the fortitude and patience of Japanese citizens will be heavily tested once the current upward cycle in the world economy comes to an end.

The apparent lack of anger amongst ordinary Japanese is all the more remarkable as their loss of relative prosperity has been both the largest except Italy's among major economies, and more prolonged than anywhere else – more than a quarter-century so far and with little let-up in sight. Moreover, the analysis here blames this on sustained dereliction and mismanagement by Japan's business, political and civil-service elite – leaving no excuse along such lines as 'nobody expected this to happen' that just about passed muster in the West back in 2009 if not later as the recovery proved feeble. The root of the problem lies in the chart overleaf:

Figure 18 **Certain private and public flows**
% of GDP, 2015

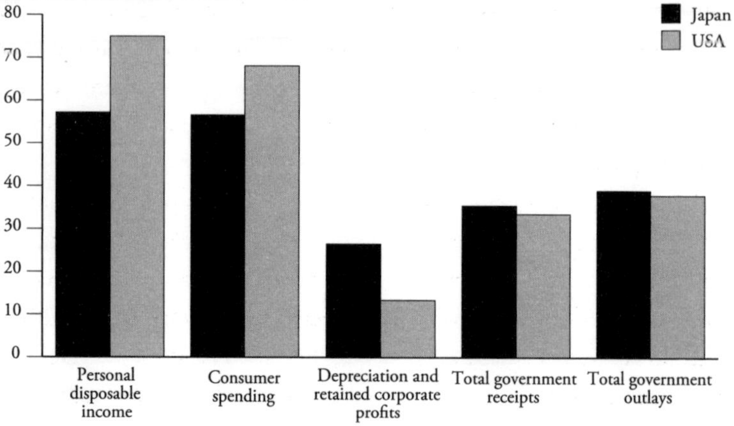

Sources: OECD, Japanese ESRI, US BEA, TS Lombard, author

The chart takes advantage of the fortuitous similarity in the size of the public sector in the US and Japan (the two sets of columns on the right-hand side of the chart). This permits direct comparison of business and household cash flows – the broad distribution of income within the private sector. As can be seen, business cash flow (depreciation plus retained profit) is twice as high in Japan as the US: 26.5% of output versus 13.3%. Unsurprisingly, the difference is reversed for after-tax (i.e. disposable) household income – 75% of GDP in the US versus 57.2% in Japan.

(The household income differential of 17.8% of GDP is greater than the 13.2% the other way for business income, a 'difference in the differences' of 4.6 percentage points. But the difference between 2015's overseas surplus of 3.1% of GDP in Japan and a deficit of 2.4% in the US is 5.5 percentage points, so aggregate disposable income flows in Japan fall short by a comparable amount.)

The argument here is that the driving force, the causative element, in this imbalance is the habit of excessive income retention in Japanese business. This surplus has been preserved at the expense of Japan's labour force. On the supply side, the protection of weak business managements by this massive cash flow is a primary reason why Japan's growth has slowed dramatically since 1990s. The country has suffered a disproportionate loss of world market share despite relative labour costs going down by nearly half versus international competitors.

On the demand side, so much income pre-empted by business causes a shortage of household spendable income. The result is insufficient consumer demand. Luckily, Japanese household savings are less than in the US (contrary to received wisdom). So the difference in consumer spending shown in Figure 18 is 11½% of GDP, less than that of disposable income. (These data, though for 2015 only, are typical of all years this century.)

A shortage of private domestic demand can only be made up by government spending or a trade surplus. Private domestic demand itself is made up of consumer spending plus capex. So insufficient consumer spending, as has occurred consistently in Japan, has to be made up either by capex or government deficit spending or a trade surplus.

Japan's capex has been consistently large, relative to its national income. This might be thought to be a 'good thing'. Capex is generally talked up as virtuous in economic commentary. But of course it represents output that is not available to satisfy people's immediate needs and desires. So such commentary praising capex, for example as provision for the future, is only valid if the capex produces genuine benefits.

The conventional idea is that more capex should cause faster economic growth. If people are putting a greater portion of income and output aside from current consumption into future provision, that should be rewarded by greater growth of output and therefore future consumable income. In general in the post-war era this has been true amongst market economies, both advanced and developing. In

Figure 19 **20-year averages of growth and capex**

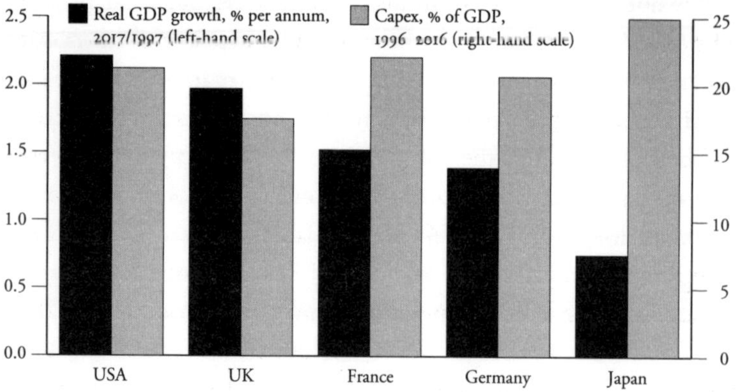

Sources: OECD, TS Lombard, author

the US, however, growth has exceeded that of most other advanced countries despite a lower share of income and output being invested.

The chart above shows clearly that the US has been getting much more 'bang for the buck' from its capex. The UK is clearly more effective than France or Germany, though equally clearly it has under-invested, as it is the only country devoting less than 20% of GDP to capex, and at 17½% quite a lot less (an important aspect of the Brexit debate in Chapter 15). Nonetheless, British growth over the past twenty years has been greater than German and French, despite much less capex.

Standing out in the chart, however, is Japan, which has grown extremely slowly, and yet with very high and clearly wasteful rates of capex. It is fine to say, as some do, that a falling population means slower growth does not necessarily result in worse income growth per head. (Though Japan fails on that count too.) But the scale of capex, much of it by public authorities trying to offset inadequate demand, has generated well-justified jokes about 'bridges to nowhere', 'vegetable airports' (to get urban shops supplied with ultra-fresh greens) and (perhaps best) 'paving Mount Fuji'.

It is not just a matter of infrastructural waste. Japanese private and public firms have also not been immune to wasteful capex out of their surfeit of saving. But the declining need for, or profitability of, private capex has helped restrain their waste, despite the negligible cost of capital of the past twenty years, i.e. very low interest rates in yen. Private capex, including housing, was still absorbing more than 20% of total output in the 1990s, but in recent years has fallen to an average below 19%. Nonetheless, business saving still far exceeds capex. For example, simply the depreciation rate of the existing capital stock has in recent years averaged between 19% and 20% of output – i.e. sufficient to finance all the fresh capex without any net private saving at all. Yet retained profits of companies have added nearly 7% of GDP to cash flow. On the demand side this is dead money.

The surplus of private saving over capex is augmented by some modest saving of households. In the post-crisis era the financial surplus of saving over capex in the private sector – households plus business – has been 8–9% of gross national output and incomes. This has to be offset by deficits elsewhere, as total net flows in an economy are always zero. Either the government has a deficit or foreigners run deficits with Japan, a roundabout way of saying that Japan has an overseas surplus. In practice, over recent years the overseas surplus has typically been nearly 3% of output, and the government deficit 6%.

The 3%-of-output surplus has been the means by which the Japanese savings glut, together with the deliberately undervalued currency, has exported its demand weakness to the rest of the world. The government deficit, including the massively wasteful infrastructure capex ('paving Mount Fuji'), has steadily raised the Japanese national debt burden relative to national income. Because the authorities have never accepted explicitly the logic expressed here,

Figure 20 **Japan: real FX rate and export market share**

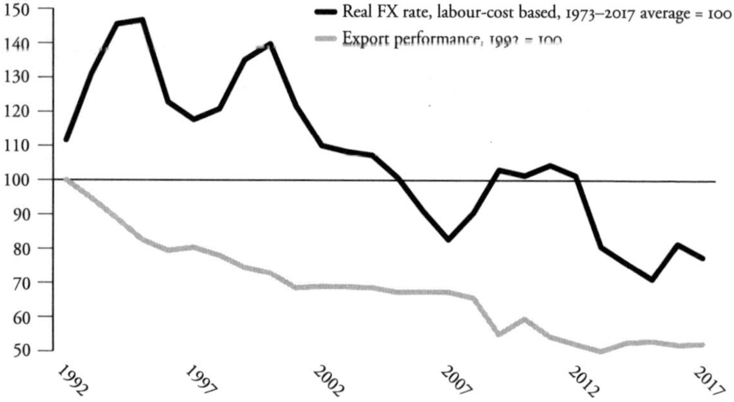

Sources: OECD, TS Lombard, author

and have a conventional aversion to a rising debt burden, periodic (and futile) efforts to shrink the budget deficit have held back aggregate demand over the years, reinforcing deflation. The weakened economy has then ensured ultra-easy monetary policies and a falling real exchange rate of the yen.

But the rest of the world, since 2008, has not been able to support Japan's lust for large overseas surpluses, so growth has been feeble, averaging ¾% a year over the past twenty years: just under ½% a year since 2007 compared with 1% in the previous ten years. But this collapse of growth from rates of 4–5% in the 1970s and 1980s is not just a function of hobbled demand. It also reflects a major worsening of business performance.

Figure 20 above illustrates the poor performance of Japanese industry over the past twenty-five years. It shows how the real value of the yen has fallen, specifically how Japanese labour costs have gone down by nearly half relative to its trading partners since the mid-1990s. Partly, this reflected clear overvaluation twenty years

Figure 21 **Export performance versus target markets**
1992 = 100

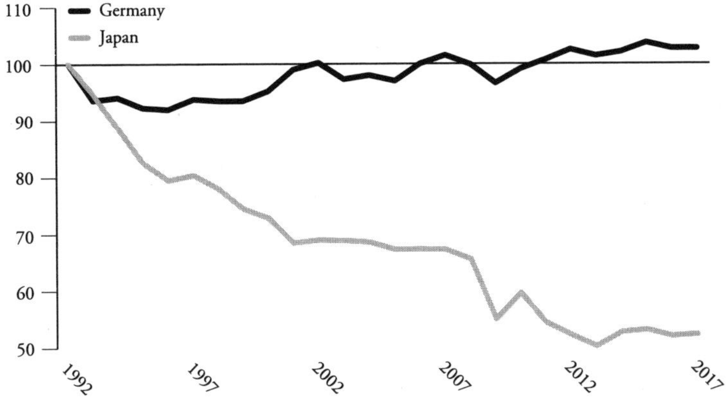

Sources: OECD, TS Lombard, author

ago. But much of the decline turns out, as we shall see, to be the financial market's recognition of worsening Japanese business management.

The clinching point is the contrast between Japan and Germany in Figure 21. This shows for each country the progress over time of its export volume (i.e. inflation adjusted) relative to the import volume of the countries to which it exports. It is a form of geographically adjusted world trade share for each country, calculated by the OECD. Germany was seriously overvalued in the mid-1990s, like Japan, and has likewise seen a major cut in its relative labour costs to a level well below its long-run average. But the German response has been positive – and conventional. It has sustained its world market share.

This German performance is remarkable as most advanced economies have lost market share. China and other emerging economies have gained. The average advanced-country loss is about 20%, as in the US and France. Germany's performance seems better than can

Figure 22 **Real FX rates**
1973–2017 average = 100

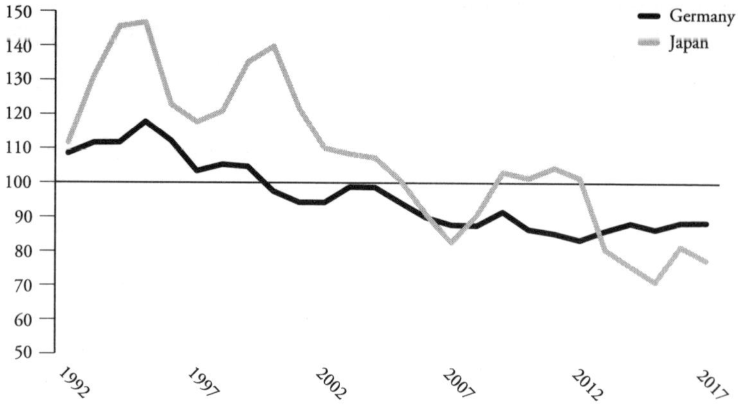

Sources: OECD, TS Lombard, author

be explained by its improved cost competitiveness, as will be seen below in looking at the EA economy (see Chapter 14). But the chief point here is that Japan's real devaluation, its gain of cost competitiveness, has been greater than Germany's, and yet its loss of world market share is only exceeded by that of ultra-uncompetitive (in every sense) Italy amongst major economies.

Conventional economic logic says that a cut in a country's real exchange rate, by making it more cost-competitive, should lead to gains in market share – or vice versa for an increase in the real exchange rate. Germany and Italy both fit within this logic. But this logic only applies if the real exchange rate is the causative factor and the market share is the result. In Japan's case, cause and effect appear reversed. It is the weakness of managements and product strategies that has forced a lower real exchange rate. In effect, Japan's goods have become so uncompetitive in specification that only by slashing the price can they be sold.

Common observation supports this conclusion. Thirty years

ago what people most wanted was Toyota or Honda cars, Nintendo GameBoys, Sony Walkmans and Sharp fax machines – all made in Japan. Nowadays, people still like the cars, though they are often more cheaply made outside Japan. But the electronics business has moved into hi-tech, led by US firms – and with the likes of Samsung in Korea also outperforming Japanese producers.

The result of this inversion of normal cause and effect is that Japanese exports have suffered in market share both in volume and price. It is highly likely that the rich cash flow in Japanese business has protected it from the cold blast of competition. But the loss of real income has not been escaped – it has simply been shifted onto the labour force, whose relative standard of living has been eroded rapidly by falling wages.

Total pay per worker has fallen at a ½% average rate over the past twenty years, and more narrowly defined wage rates by ¾%, while output per worker has been rising by ¾%. This disparity has been offset by a mix of a rising share of business saving and, more importantly, the falling relative value of Japanese exports. From the standpoint of Japanese people, after-tax income per head was just over two-thirds that of US people at comparable prices in the mid-1990s (i.e. with exchange rates adjusted for domestic price differences). But it has been ten percentage points lower in recent years, a decline of more than one-seventh in relative income.

The two human factors that seem to underpin this sorry tale of national decline are the cushioned complacency of the business elite and the docility and deference of the labour force. Is either likely to change?

Apart from the sheer comfort of their position, Japanese managements are locked into undue retention of cash by Japan's industrial structure. Two-fifths of company shares are owned by other companies, who also control the investments and cash flow of pension assets that account for nearly another fifth of the stock market's capitalisation. More than a fifth of the shares are held by foreigners, who are largely passive. That leaves only one-fifth in the hands of individual shareholders. If the cash flow were to be paid out as dividends (or share buybacks) most of it would remain under corporate control, with a significant portion going abroad.

Radical changes in Japanese corporate law and/or tax incentives might bring about a reduction in business's cash-hoarding tendency; these have been proposed in certain circles. But the problems and tendencies described here have been known for years – decades, in fact – without any serious action in prospect. The Liberal Democratic party that has mostly formed Japanese governments (including the current one) is very much beholden to business interests, so it is unrealistic to expect any major changes to current business behaviour in the absence of some big change in world or Japanese domestic conditions.

Will Japanese labour start to fight back against the relative decline of its standard of living? On one side of the argument, the Japanese standard of living remains far and away the highest in Asia, even if by a lesser margin than twenty years ago. By way of comparison, the very high standard of living in Sweden in the late 1940s after World War II, relative to other European countries but also even the United States, fell steadily for thirty years before Swedish people started to get restive about this decline from the late 1970s onward.

Of course, Japan's relative decline is in a much less buoyant global context than Sweden's in the 1950s, 1960s and early 1970s. It therefore comes close to absolute decline, rather than just a slower rate of gain than elsewhere. And the performance relative to other Asian countries, whose growth since the financial crisis has outpaced that of the developed West, is more clearly negative. Also, the parallel sustenance of a cosseted, 'fat-cat' business elite might be a source of resentment. The story is very much one of divergent income shares. While the pressure on middle-income people reflects different forces in Japan than in the West, it raises the same question of how long it can last without provoking social or political trouble.

As well as how long the relegation of labour interests can be sustained, a salient question for Japan is how long government deficits at 6% of national output can be sustained. For now, Japan's traditional ways are working well enough. Ultra-low (in fact, negative) interest rates are just succeeding in restraining the yen's exchange rate, which is on the other hand buoyed by the large current-account surplus, and attractive stock markets as profits soar. Currently healthy world trade perfectly suits Japan, which is a tag-along economy. But 2014's attempt to shrink the deficit with a consumption-tax increase provoked renewed, if slight, recession. The cyclical low point for the deficit – 2015's 3½% of GDP, down from the 2009 peak of 9¾% – was quickly obviated by fiscal stimulus, and it was back to 4¾% in 2017 despite good growth.

Probably, the world will not let Japan enjoy a sustained current-account surplus even as large as 3% of GDP, and the current 4% is highly unlikely to last. The yen too easily appreciates at the first sign of trouble, and huge Japanese surpluses tend to boost it, as well as making trouble elsewhere. The private sector financial surplus is unlikely to shift sustainably below 8% of GDP; 9% could remain the long-run average. So the budget deficit is destined to fluctuate around 6%. This would only cease to be true if the government seriously increased the tax burden on business, not households – either by raising the corporate tax rate (already a high 32%), reducing deductions (e.g. for depreciation) or by some other means. There is little sign of this being proposed even, let alone enacted.

A long-standing question has been how long Japan can continue to run up debts, with the budget in apparently permanent deficit. Gross government debt has risen since 2000 from 130% of output to 220%. The Japanese government controls substantial financial assets, so the net debt is a better measure of its liabilities. This has increased from 47% of output in 2000 to 130% in 2017, only a slightly smaller increase than in the gross debt ratio. Japan's government debt is higher than Greece's at the time of its initial crisis in early 2010. How long can this last?

Pessimists have lost money betting on a Japanese debt crisis for much of this century. They have mostly 'retired hurt' at this point. While foreigners have a portion of Japan's zero-yield debt, most of it is owned by Japanese investors, who appear to have unlimited faith in their government, or at least in 'Japan, Inc.'.

Treating the 130% debt/output figure as the most representative, the dilemma for Japan is that a 6%-of-output budget deficit will tend to raise the debt ratio rapidly unless the growth of output at current prices is fast enough to hold down the ratio. Only that way can the extra debt from 'this year's' deficit be offset by the larger output and income over which the prior debt can be stretched.

Without imposing algebra, the growth of current-price output needed to hold the ratio at today's 130% (i.e. 1.3) is 6% divided by 1.3, i.e. about 4½%. But as the real growth trend of Japan is only ½% a year, current-price growth of 4½% would require 4% inflation. If inflation were less – and it has been less, mostly negative, for the past quarter-century – then the current-price growth of output would be less than 4½% and the debt ratio would grow from 130%. This is the likely outcome.

The choice for Japan, given the size of the budget deficits needed to offset excessive and unneeded business saving, is either a permanently escalating debt ratio or a shift into inflation at 4%, twice the (admittedly arbitrary) target of 2%. In reality, Japanese habits – especially wage restraint – are inimical to the generation of inflation. A continued increase in the debt ratio is the most likely outcome. When this reaches crisis proportions is anyone's guess, but at some stage it will. Meanwhile, Japanese people, like Westerners, are subject to real income stress, as well as elite incompetence and rising inequality. Whether and when they will cut up rough remains to be seen.

13

Can China dodge the 'middle-income trap'?

Japan and Korea are the chief non-Western countries (excluding the Singapore and Hong Kong city-states) to have vaulted out of developing-country, emerging-market status. The middle-income trap is exemplified by Brazil, sometimes sarcastically referred to as 'the country of the future for the past fifty years'. Brazil's output and income per head at comparable prices peaked at 38% of the US in 1980, and has fallen back ever since: the ratio is now 26%.

Japan peaked at 85% of US output per head in 1991, and is now back to 72%. Korea has generally been behind Japan. In 1997, just before the Asian crisis, it had reached 44% of the US level, but after the 1998 crisis and fallback it rose steadily to reach a 66% ratio by 2017, close to Japan's 72%. So the catch-up process has not been stopped in a 'middle-income trap' in Korea. It may never be.

China's real GDP growth rate was nearly 10% in the years until 2011, after which it slowed. Its output per head of population rose from 2.5% of the US in 1980 to 20.7% in 2011 (all at comparable prices). Since then the catch-up has been less rapid proportionately, but by 2017 the ratio reached 28%, having passed Brazil's in 2016. With growth expected to continue at 6% a year for the next few years and the US growing at 1½–2%, this ratio could rise to the mid-30s in five years.

There is nothing in the current situation or prospects of China

Figure 23 **Chinese growth slowdown achieved, but debt escalated**

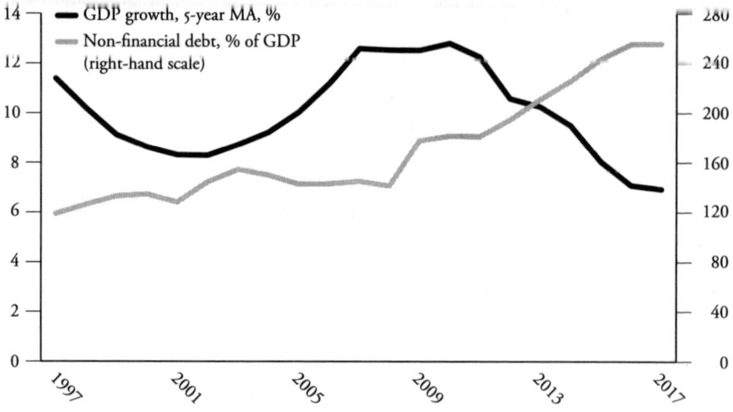

Sources: CEIC, BIS, TS Lombard, author

to suggest this is unachievable. The chief medium-term adjustments needed are a lesser dependence of growth on escalating debt, and a sustained reduction in recent grotesquely high ratios of saving and investment to total output and incomes. The two are connected. The combination of very high business saving in well-run (and also often monopolistic) parts of the Chinese economy with wasteful investment elsewhere has caused debt to escalate. With few portfolio investment opportunities in China, and controls on capital exports, profits tend to be banked. The banks then lend the money, often under government instruction (implicitly or explicitly), to politically mandated, wasteful projects.

Reduction of capex waste has clearly started, though it has a long way to go. The ratio of debt to output has stabilised in recent quarters at levels well below those of countries in difficulties – in fact, below the ratios typical in developed economies generally, though above those of other emerging economies. Broad money (M2) has slowed to about an 8½% growth rate, roughly in line with nominal

GDP. So debt is no longer rising faster than GDP. This is partly caused by China slowing to 6% growth in a year in which the world at large is growing faster than usual. The debt ratio may start to rise again when the world economy slows – perhaps late in 2019 and 2020. But the massive debt escalation of 2011–16 now seems past.

It is reasonable to regard China's supercharged growth in the early post-Mao period as similar to the improvement a person feels when they stop banging their head against a brick wall: the end of Chairman Mao's reign made rapid growth almost inevitable, so long as the country did not dissolve into chaos. This governance issue came to a head in 1989 with the Tiananmen Square crisis, and its violent suppression. For a year or two the direction of China became questionable, and a fallback into 'Maoist' top-down rigidity loomed. But the 'retirement' of paramount leader Deng Xiaoping in early 1992, followed by his springtime 'southern tour', reset economic policy onto a liberal path. The political supremacy of the Communist Party was retained, despite distinctly non-socialist economic policies. Deng remained paramount leader until his death in 1997.

Growth soared well over a 10% rate in 1992–5, stayed close to 10% in 1996–7, very much aided by a major devaluation in 1994, and only fell back to 8% or so in 1998–2001 despite the Asian crisis. The worst dangers from that crisis were offset by China's highly competitive, post-devaluation exchange rate. (Some analysts say that it was China's 1994 devaluation that put decisive pressure on the other Asian Tigers, helping to cause the 1997–8 crisis.) In this period, the national savings rate of close to 40% of output and incomes was on the high side, even for a developing economy, and capex was not far behind, averaging more than 35% of output. But they were within range of normal ratios; anyhow China was not yet large enough for its imbalances to be globally significant.

The run-up to the 2007–9 financial crisis changed all that. For China the start of this century had three distinct periods: up to 2004, 2005–8 and 2009–11. A combination of strong exports as the world recovered from the 2001 slowdown with rapidly growing domestic capex led to an overheated economy by 2004. Capex rose from 34.3% of output in 2000 to 42.7% in 2004. Yet the trade surplus was sustained at 2½% of output despite booming domestic demand. As domestic demand was restrained in 2005–6, net exports jumped to 7½% of output, even though the previously fixed yuan exchange rate was allowed to appreciate from July 2005. All-out export and domestic expansion in 2007 took this trade surplus up to 8½%, while GDP jumped by more than 14% even on the official data, and by 16% on the recalculation of real Chinese GDP developed at Lombard Street Research (now part of TS Lombard).

On this recalculated basis, real output was still up 9% from the year-before quarter as late as the third quarter of 2008 (when the Beijing Olympics took place). But September 2008's onset of full-scale global financial crisis saw China's exports plummet; before then developed economies had been in recession for a couple of quarters but not yet in crisis. Real output scarcely grew in the winter quarters for the first time on record in the post-Mao era, though a proper recalculation of quarterly growth (sadly impossible) might have produced a negative quarter or two after the Tiananmen crisis of mid-1989.

China was the first major economy to engage in massive stimulus in response to the financial crisis. Its huge spending programme, announced in December 2008, caused real domestic demand to rise at a near-20% annual rate for five quarters between the last quarter of 2008 and the first of 2010. The good news was that this spread enormous stimulus throughout the world, and helped spur global recovery. The bad news was that the nature of the stimulus embedded the imbalances that caused major Chinese and global difficulties in 2012–15.

The imbalances had been brewing well before the crisis. The major undervaluation of China's yuan from 1994 on started to inflate the trade surplus and business profits once the Asian crisis was over. For a while, in the overheating period to 2004, the decline of the personal income share of GDP was matched by booming capex. But once capex restraint came into play in 2005 soaring exports took over. The share of national output taken by disposable personal income fell from 66% in 2000 to 58% in 2007. Yet personal savings went up vis-à-vis personal income. So consumer spending fell over the same seven years, from 46% of output to 36%. The government spending share was also down by three percentage points. The capex share was up by seven percentage points and the trade surplus by six.

The result by 2007 was an economy where saving took an unprecedented 50% of output, with capex also unreasonably large at 41%. The 9% difference was the huge trade surplus. When the crisis led to exports collapsing, the Chinese authorities, rightly (from a Keynesian standpoint) wanting domestic spending to offset this export weakness, made the wrong choice. They should have sought ways of reducing the absurd, in fact grotesque, 50% savings rate. Instead, they inflated the already seriously wasteful investment rate of 41%.

The reason for this choice was simple. The government could instruct the state-owned banks that dominated the economy to lend, and provincial governments to drum up projects that the lending could finance. Getting ordinary Chinese to save less was altogether less likely to succeed. So the savings rate in the economy stayed at 2007's 50% or more through until 2013. The capex share rose to 48% in 2010. It has stayed just under the savings rate ever since.

Several consequences followed from this massive surge of China's 'metal-bashing' and construction. Wages inflated at the same time that the yuan appreciated, rendering China uncompetitive in costs by 2011–12. The excessive rate of investment created overcapacity in many industries, undermining the profitability of existing plants both in China and elsewhere. The return on assets in Chinese non-financial businesses had been falling even before the crisis, when the

Figure 24 **Chinese non-financial companies, net income as % of total assets**

Sources: Datastream, TS Lombard, author

capex rate was about 41% of GDP. Its rise to 48% inevitably eroded returns further.

Different people have different stories about spectacular Chinese waste – newly built cities that nobody lives in, twice as much electricity-generating capacity relative to output as in European countries, etc. But the chart above, showing for non-financial Chinese companies the ratio of net income to total assets, illustrates the point well enough. With the return on assets (RoA) around 2–3%, justification for any capex at all becomes hard to see. With the one-year loan rate at 4.35% and non-food CPI inflation now under 2%, the real cost of money – the interest rate minus the inflation rate – equals or exceeds the RoA. And that refers to total assets; with the long-run decline in the RoA, the marginal return on any given added asset is less than the average, and well below the real interest rate.

Given the pace of advance of the Chinese economy, and the rapid improvement of people's standard of living, the problem of waste caused little anxiety amongst the authorities in the 2009–15 period.

Figure 25 **Chinese non-financial debt**
% of GDP

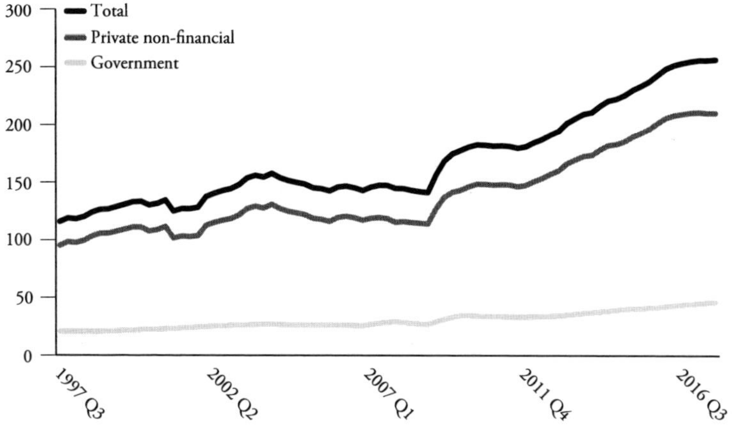

Sources: BIS, TS Lombard, author

A popular line of argument by apologists for the regime has been that the build-up of the country's infrastructure is essential to long-term development, so that poor immediate returns do not matter. Similar cavalier attitudes to the productivity of new capital spending are a major reason why no major country in the world comes close to matching US incomes per head. But it is certainly true that at current income levels, with China only 28% of the US on a comparable-price basis, further catch-up does not depend on maximal efficiency of new capex. In that sense, the authorities' 'benign neglect' has been relatively harmless, provided it does not persist too long.

What has attracted comment and concern is the run-up of debt associated with excessive capex. The data in the chart above are misleading, as 'private' debt includes debts of many entities closely associated with provincial governments. It frequently reflects loans made by state-owned banks, in many cases mandated by the authorities. In truth, the entire debt is owed by 'China, Inc.'

The upswing in 2009 reflected December 2008's stimulus programme, but the increase that started in 2011 reflected the combination of wasteful capex, slower growth and a fully valued, arguably overvalued, exchange rate. In the five years from end-2011 to end-2016, the total debt ratio went up from 180% of output to 255%, an increase of fifteen percentage points each year. This could not go on for long.

If the businesses making the best profits were the ones doing the new capex, the debt ratio would not have risen as it did. But the allocation of capital by China's banks has often followed political instructions, and has also involved major support for 'zombie' loans, where the borrower is borrowing to pay the interest, causing an unproductive run-up of debt. The current level of China's debt, 256% of output, is well below the levels in, for example, Japan. But it strongly suggests the inherent wastefulness of the capex splurge since 2009.

Fast global growth since late 2016 is enabling China to grow at a satisfactory rate without such excessive dependence on extra debt, whose ratio to output levelled off during 2017. Also, the badly needed process of shifting growth away from capex towards consumers has got under way since 2014. The share of capex in output fell from 46.8% in 2014 to 44.4% in 2017, while consumer spending went up, from 37.5% to 39.1%, with government current spending also raising its share.

The Chinese authorities seem to be serious about measures to reduce excessive saving and capex. Various forms of social welfare, concerning health and pensions, are being enhanced, reducing the pressure to save against standard ills: losing your health, losing your job and getting old. With the *hukou* system still very much in place, restricting labour mobility as well as entitlement to social benefits, the personal savings rate is likely to stay high. But from a peak of 42% of disposable income in 2010, the portion of household disposable income saved fell to 37% in 2015, and should continue downward.

Figure 26 **Real GDP growth**
% YoY, with TS Lombard recalculation

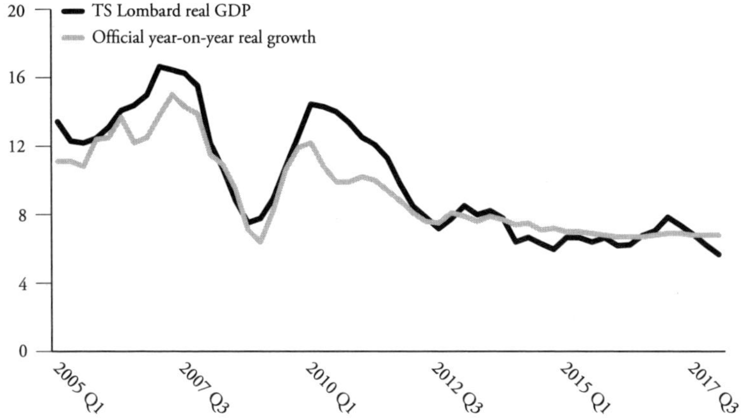

Sources: CEIC, TS Lombard, author

On the capex and waste front, unduly polluting steel plants, and other metal-bashing excesses, have been closed down. More importantly, falling RoA means that the incentive to create new assets is weakening all the time. And the high-end housing boom has also been cut back to more reasonable proportions as Chinese private investors have been chastened by the bursting of a stock market bubble in mid-2015, followed by official constraints on exporting private capital overseas, backed by the formidable 'reign of terror' in the guise of a corruption purge.

The acknowledgement of limits to Chinese economic achievements is crucial to deflating overweening ideas about China's ability to deviate from economic norms. In the aftermath of the financial crisis, with the euro area in continuing crisis, China's ability to generate investment-led growth turned it into the great hope for global investors. Whether one uses the evidently 'massaged' real growth estimates of the government, or the more realistic recalculation of TS Lombard, the turning point towards slower growth was clearly

2011. Not coincidentally, energy and commodity prices peaked in 2011 and the renewed upswing in the debt/output ratio started that year. Whereas growth in the ten years or so to 2011 was significantly faster than 10% a year, it has since then been at 6½–7%, with a cyclical low in 2015.

Delusions of Chinese omnipotence lasted for several years after 2011, despite steady deflation of stock market prices. The government connived in triggering a stock market bubble from spring 2014, and the Shanghai market went up 150% over the subsequent year, from around 2,000 on the Shanghai Composite index to more than 5,000 in June 2015. A well-justified fit of nerves then brought it down 30% to 3,500, after which the government intervened to protect investors to whom it had earlier tipped the wink in generating the bubble. The market has stagnated in the 3,000–3,500 range since then.

This awareness of limits in China – both by the authorities and by Chinese and global investors – is reinforced in helping the economy form a base for further progress by the consolidation in power of Xi Jinping, notably at and since the five-yearly Party Congress in autumn 2017. A feature of this was his reference to the need to satisfy China's own middle-income people, and this remains a spur to the social welfare improvements referred to above.

A less obvious point is that less wasteful capex makes the rebalancing of the Chinese economy relatively benign. In general, any rebalancing of an economy tends to be accompanied by slower growth. In today's China, a shift of emphasis downward in capex that accounts for 44% of GDP is hard to reconcile with growth sustained at the 6½–7% rate of the past six years. If an element accounting for 44% of GDP weakens, then incomes throughout the economy are affected, potentially multiplying the negative effect on demand. On this basis, people have tended to forecast medium-term Chinese growth as 5–6%, or even as low as 4%.

But there are offsetting factors. Most obviously, the savings rate

Figure 27 **Steadily less reliance on monetary growth since the crisis**
%

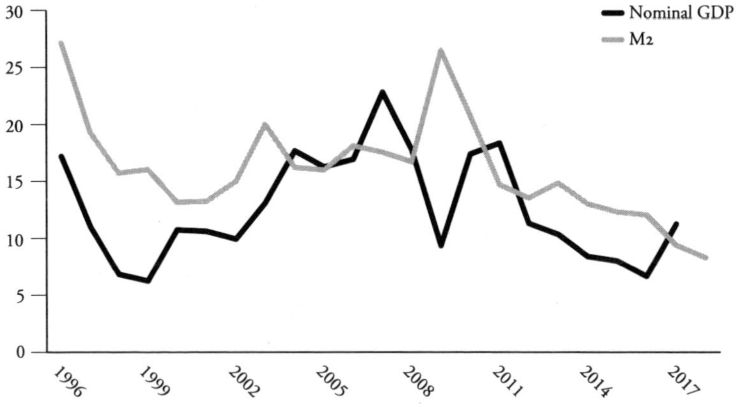

Sources: CEIC, Datastream, TS Lombard, author

in the economy is falling as fast as the capex rate. This idea can be inverted to illustrate that slower growth will not harm middle incomes. The starting point is that the dive in the consumer spending share of GDP in the years to 2011 already meant its growth rate in real terms was two percentage points less than that of total output. So 10% output growth meant 8% annual real consumer spending growth, about 7½% per head after allowing for population growth.

But the increase in the consumer-spending share of GDP in recent years has been adding two percentage points to its real growth rate compared to GDP. Even if real GDP growth drops to 5%, the real growth rate of consumer spending could be 7%, i.e. 6½% a head. But this is operating from a higher base, and with less 'corruption' of income in their favour by the 'elite cadres'. The outlook for middle incomes is thus benign, despite the likely slowdown of growth. If the medium-term real GDP growth rate turns out to be 6%, as we expect at TS Lombard, there would be no slowdown at all in consumer growth.

The shift of the Chinese supply side from metal-bashing to services and hi-tech, and of the demand side from wasteful capex to consumer demand, is matched by a lesser dependence on rapidly growing money supply – the counterpart of bank lending, which accounts for the bulk of debt growth. The future growth of broad money is likely to remain in the 8% region, which is consistent with real output growth at 6% and 2–3% inflation, without implying any premium growth of credit vis-à-vis incomes.

The strange conclusion of all this is that the question of whether China will fall into the middle-income trap does not for now require an answer. The current momentum and rebalancing of China should enable it to grow in five years from its 2017 ratio of 27% of the US income per head to about 34% in 2022. While there will be upsets along the way, and China could also be victim of a major global economic crisis – which seems unlikely, but is always possible – both debt-ratio stabilisation and the needed rebalancing seem likely to be achieved.

With about four times the US population, a projection of real incomes of one-third at comparable prices means the Chinese economy could be a third larger than the US by 2022. This dawning reality is causing major anxiety in the US, and a degree of triumphalism in China that could lead to political consequences – 'geopolitical' consequences, to use the polite word for war. But the analysis in this book can do no more than describe the possible context of that, not its form. From the standpoint of economic analysis, and the populism encountered elsewhere, China is not a medium-term problem.

14

Euro Area – growing now, but still divergent

On a global analysis, the EA recovery since 2014, like Japan's, has depended on much lower oil and other commodity prices. The EA by 2013–14, after a double-dip recession caused by the euro crisis, was running a near-$400 billion current-account surplus – over $500 billion including Switzerland, Sweden and Denmark,

Figure 28 **Current account balances**
$ billion

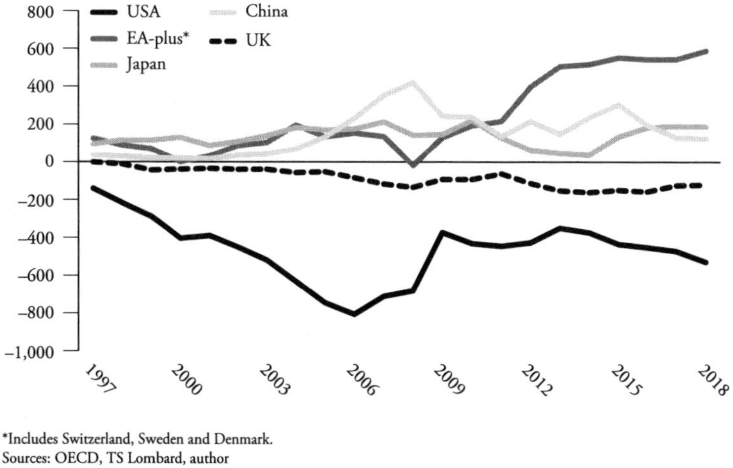

*Includes Switzerland, Sweden and Denmark.
Sources: OECD, TS Lombard, author

which are integral to the north-central Europe (NCE) economy. Germany's surplus alone was more than $250 billion, and the rest were in surplus or balance after years of tight fiscal policy. For this surplus economy to devalue to create export-led growth – which was essentially what ECB policy under Draghi amounted to – was globally anti-social, to put it at a minimum. (The same can be said of Abenomics phase 2 in Japan, which also started in mid-2014. But Japan is a smaller and less healthy economy than continental western Europe.)

Global damage was avoided, because the pain was taken by cash-glutted oil and other commodity producers, not traditional deficit countries, particularly the US. Between 2013 and 2015 the current account of oil-producing countries alone moved from a surplus of $700 billion to a deficit of $200 billion, a $900 billion shift that was more than 1% of world output. The overall shift was much greater, when other commodity producers and oil producers in the US such as shale frackers are included. Sharp cutbacks by these people accounted for the bulk of the mid-decade slowdown in 2015 – humans respond to pain much faster than to gain. The 2015 slowdown also reflected the weakness of China and the soaring US dollar (mirror image of the devaluing euro and yen).

The EA was lucky, however, and as a result has enjoyed five straight years of good recovery since early 2013. Normally, a devaluation helps business – via better exports and profits – but harms households, because of the rise in import prices that is the normal result of devaluation. But the collapse of oil and other commodity prices outweighed the rise of import prices for EA households in late 2014 and early 2015, so the sharp recovery of consumer spending did not slacken.

That Europe is the largest source of OPEC imports, and also of the former Soviet Union, meant that the devaluation was not immediately effective in raising export volumes, but the current-account surplus of continental western Europe (excluding oil-country

Figure 29 **EA car sales**
Monthly

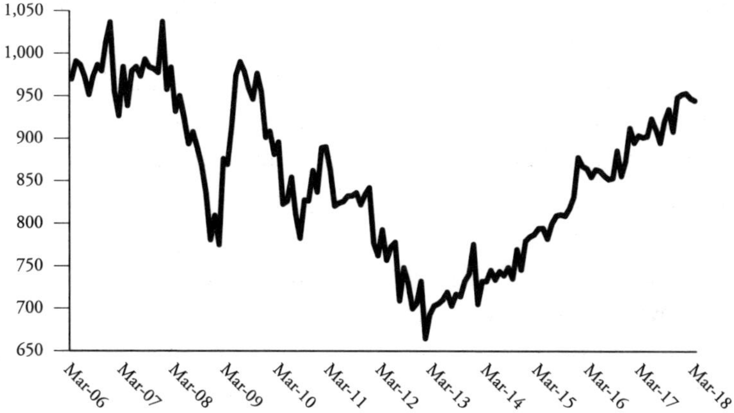

Sources: Datastream, TS Lombard, author

Figure 30 **EA retail volume**
2010 = 100

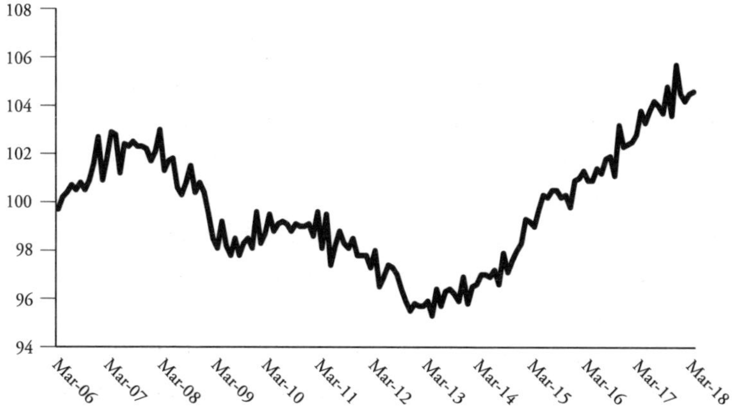

Sources: Datastream, TS Lombard, author

Figure 31 **North-central Europe (NCE) and other GDP**
$ billion, 2016 current prices

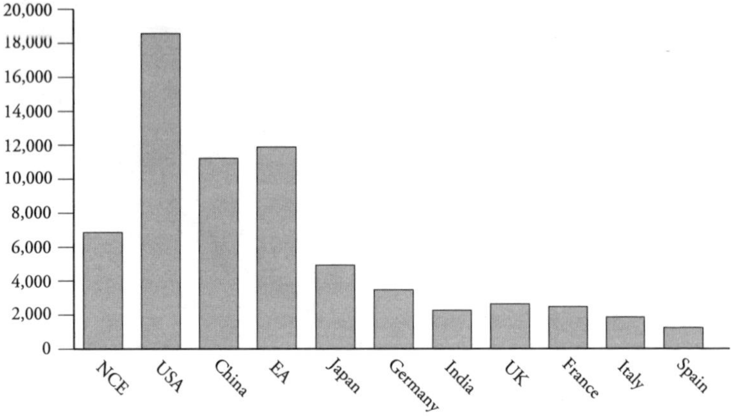

Sources: OECD, TS Lombard, author

Norway) rose from $500 billion in 2013 to $550 billion 2015. It held steady for 2016–17 as rapid growth sucked in imports, matching export growth, but is likely to expand to $600 billion in 2018 as the world economy booms and the euro remains undervalued.

While the EA is a single economy as regards monetary policy, it is essential to deal with individual countries and regional links to understand what has happened, as well as its prospects. Germany, for example, has much greater links with Switzerland, which is not in the EU let alone the EA, than with Spain, one of the four larger EA economies. Figure 31 isolates the NCE economy, German-centred western Europe. This includes (to the north) Scandinavia excluding Norway, (to the west) Holland, Belgium and Luxembourg ('Benelux'), and (to the south) Switzerland and Austria. In aggregate these German neighbours have the same output as Germany. Over time, Poland, the Czech Republic and maybe other central-eastern ex-Comecon countries are becoming part of this bloc.

The NCE economy of about $7 trillion is clearly well behind

the US ($19 trillion) and China ($13 trillion) but larger than Japan's $5 trillion (all at current prices and exchange rates in 2016). In the European context it is nearly three times France and Britain (both $2½ trillion), nearly four times Italy's $1.8 trillion and six times Spain's $1.2 trillion. Its prospective current-account surplus is more than $550 billion, with modest surpluses in France, Italy, Spain, etc., augmenting this to $600 billion for continental western Europe. This only begins to hint at the imbalances in the EA, because it does not differentiate between relatively balanced and healthy conditions in France and Spain, versus serious problems in Italy (and Greece).

The differential between German and Italian growth over the ten years since the start of the crisis is 18%, since German output is up 12% from its pre-crisis peak, whereas Italy's is still down 6%. Even before the crisis, when Germany was being unduly deflated in 2002–5 by Hans Eichel, its growth exceeded Italy's. French growth has also fallen short of Germany's, though it is less unbalanced. French households have done better than Germans in real after-tax income over the life of the euro (i.e. since 1998). With the EA economy increasingly dominated by the progress of NCE, France has to continue its integration with Germany. The new Macron presidency is likely to carry out the liberalising reforms that entails.

Spain went through a traumatic process of unbalanced expansion in 1999–2007, followed by major depression and labour-cost adjustment in 2008–13, and then a resumption of fast growth. Unemployment was more than 20% of the labour force from 2010 to 2016, and during those six years it averaged 23%. This violent austerity led to a major cut in its labour costs – including large falls in nominal wages – and the resulting cost competitiveness has permitted Spain, as growth resumed from early 2013, to diverge radically from Italy, as Figure 32 shows.

Spain enjoyed balanced growth at about 4% in real terms from the Barcelona Olympics (1992) to the start of the euro (1999), with

Figure 32 **Real GDP**
2008 Q1 (pre-crisis peak) = 100

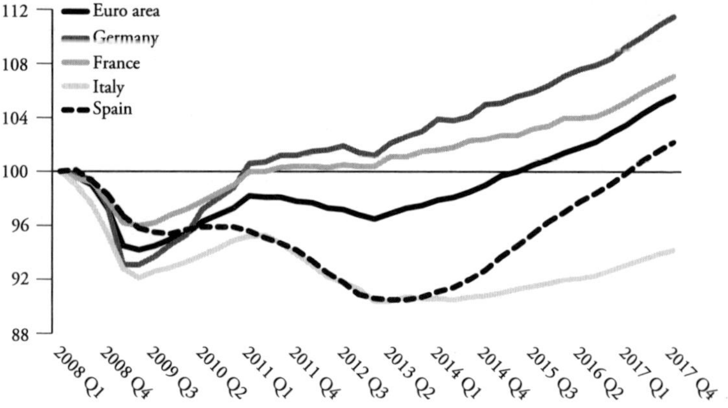

Sources: Datastream, TS Lombard, author

inflation also in the 4% region. Under the euro it kept to the same real growth and inflation, but increasingly based on debt-financed construction and real estate activity. Its cost basis became rapidly uncompetitive for international trade, but its interest rates – essentially set in Germany – were far too low for an economy in its condition, provoking the unbalanced upsurge.

The gross imbalances built up in 2000–7 were unwound by the 2008–13 trauma. Having adjusted and restored competitiveness with such pain it is highly unlikely that Spain will accede to soft-pedalling of austerity programmes for any country that hits trouble in future, as is likely for Italy and Greece.

Figure 33 shows labour-cost competitiveness in the four major EA economies. Each is measured vis-à-vis its own appropriate long-run average: for Germany, France and Italy this means the forty-five years since the breakdown of Bretton Woods fixed exchange rates in 1973, while for Spain the average is since 1992, and for the EA since 1995. Since the OECD developed these estimates the euro's real

Figure 33 **Relative unit labour costs**
Long-run average = 100

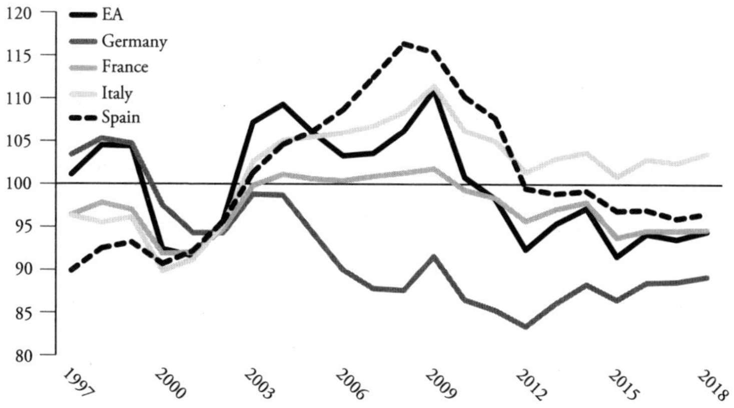

Sources: OECD, TS Lombard, author

exchange rate is up rather over 1%, so on this labour-cost basis it is 4–5% undervalued. On the basis of relative producer prices (as used in the JP Morgan real FX indices) it is still undervalued, but by less.

The striking point is that despite very restrained Italian wage gains since the crisis, the relative labour-cost differential between Italy and Germany remains 14–15%. Right now this problem is in abeyance, because Germany being 11% undervalued means Italy is only about 3–4% overvalued. And the Italian economy is pulled along by its links to booming Germany. But that is simply the temporary result of the ECB's ultra-easy monetary policy, which though nominally governed by the inflation target ('under but close to 2%') is in reality designed to protect Italy. In all likelihood, the euro will appreciate back to a more neutral position in which Germany is much less undervalued and Italy much more overvalued – as was the case pre-crisis. Quite probably, given the huge current-account surplus, the euro will even become overvalued.

The background to Italy's troubles is not just the euro, but the conduct of its economic policy in the previous three decades, and the eruption onto the world scene of China over the twenty years from the mid-1990s. For decades before joining the euro Italy allowed major restrictive practices and other obstacles to market forces to persist. It solved the problem of generating growth by frequent devaluation of the lira.

One effect of this policy of competing largely on price was that Italy's industrial structure became increasingly focused on industries where price was the decisive factor, not firm-specific value added – i.e. commodity industries such as textiles, iron and steel, tiles, etc. These are, of course, precisely the industries in which entry-level developing economies launch their efforts to achieve modernity. So Italy fixed its exchange rate by means of euro membership at precisely the point when massive Chinese competition, heavily focused on cheap costs and prices, was becoming most intense. Large swathes of Italian industry were wiped out as Italy's relative costs rose in 2000–9 to more than 10% above its long-run average.

Italy has a deeper problem – weakness of the legal system. In a lawsuit the aggrieved party is unlikely to be compensated in current Italian conditions within ten years. For businesses this means personal trust is a precondition of willingness to act. In turn this tends to lead to smaller, family-run businesses, operating on a local basis. However excellent such smaller firms may be, economies of scale and the advantages of international reach are often absent. Italy has also been laggard in exploiting hi-tech. Large-scale businesses are often government-owned and subject to the notorious inefficiency and political meddling of Italy's public sector. Italy's businesses have thus become relatively provincial in part because of the weak legal system, which is unlikely to change much in future.

Spain's cost experience was even worse, pre-crisis – its relative costs were more than 15% too high by 2008–9. But Spain maintained its world market share remarkably well during the build-up to the crisis, despite its increasing cost disadvantage. And then between

2008 and 2012, Spain cut its costs so drastically that it shifted to marginal undervaluation from more than 15% overvaluation.

There is no sign whatever of Italian supply-side policies changing to achieve a similar result, nor of a willingness to impose the type of austerity that was applied in Spain. On the contrary, with the new German coalition talking of fiscal stimulus – despite the EA's growth now being above-potential and its rising inflation far from any danger of deflation – fiscal stimulus is also likely in Italy, whatever coalition government emerges after the recent elections.

The point is that Spain's crisis was a dynamic private-sector collapse, whereas Italy's was and is a moribund public-sector seize-up. Spain never had a fiscal problem. For all Germany's talk of the need for fiscal responsibility – Stability and Growth Pact, Fiscal Compact, etc. – in the five pre-crisis years 2003–7 Germany ran an average budget deficit of 2½% of output while Spain ran an average budget *surplus* of 1%. Spain's crisis had nothing to do with fiscal irresponsibility, and everything to do with the wrongness of being in the euro with grossly inappropriate interest rates for Spanish circumstances.

The sad reality is that Italy, with all the rigidities in its society and economy, is yoked in the euro with countries that are likely to grow well for a number of years alongside an appreciating currency. This means a fresh, if lesser, euro crisis is likely sometime in 2019–22. For the genesis of that we have to look at NCE, not only Germany, Austria, Belgium and the Netherlands, which are all in the EA, but also Switzerland, Sweden and Denmark.

The comparison between Germany and most of the rest of the EA is clear – Germany did much worse before the crisis and much better afterwards. But the non-German parts of NCE have had the best (or 'least worst') of both worlds, especially Sweden and Switzerland. They did fine before the crisis and have largely matched Germany since, although less so during Germany's particularly strong performance in 2010–11 as China rocketed out of recession on a wave of capex, much of it using German kit.

In the first decade of the euro's existence, NCE economies grew less than other continental countries, partly because of the latter being inflated by the imbalances – notably, euro interest rates being much too low in their conditions – and partly because Germany, to which they were so closely linked, was subjected to heavy fiscal deflation in 2002–5.

In the latest ten years to 2017, NCE has much outperformed other continental countries, even with Spain recovering to a real growth rate of 3%-plus. The post-crisis period has seen plenty of divergence within these two groups. In NCE, two non-euro economies, Sweden and Switzerland, have done significantly better than Germany and especially Holland. The other non-euro economy, Denmark, has done worse, not least because it shadowed the euro with the Danish crown, rather than floating its currency independently like the other two. But within the EA, the smaller north-central economies, Austria, Belgium, Finland and the Netherlands, have also underperformed Germany, though over the whole life of the euro they are still ahead.

There is similar divergence of performance since the crisis in other EA countries. The significance of this lies in the likely scenarios for future EA imbalances, rather than directly affecting likely NCE growth. In the post-crisis period, with the euro crisis causing a double-dip recession in 2012–13, the dividing line was roughly north versus south (excluding Ireland's role in the 'periphery'). But future tensions in the EA are unlikely to involve Spain. With Spain and NCE likely to grow consistently, it is only Italy (and Greece and possibly Portugal) that are potentially in trouble through being yoked to Germany.

Demographics are supposedly stable and predictable, but this has not been true of NCE in recent years. The classic case is Germany, but the pattern of labour force and employment growth being strong for the whole of this century, and even more so since 2010, is fairly consistent across NCE. Countries with some slowing post-2010 compared to previously are Holland, Belgium and Finland – all in

Figure 34 **Labour-force growth**
% pa, actual versus forecast

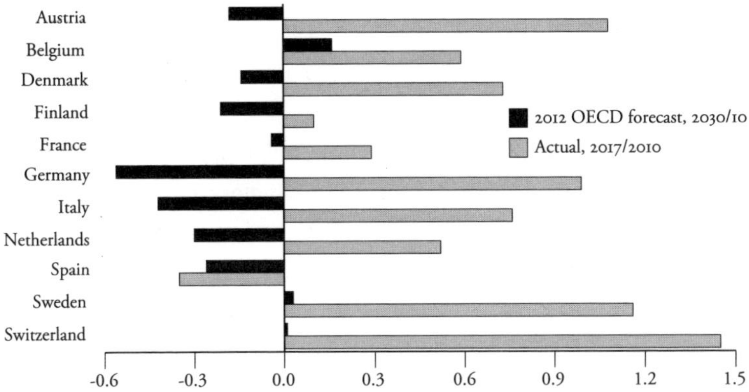

Sources: OECD, TS Lombard, author

the euro, unlike the three non-euro members, which have all shown very healthy labour-force growth rates, faster than Germany's in the case of Sweden and Switzerland. Figure 34 contrasts annual growth over the seven years 2011–17 with the OECD's 2012 forecast for the twenty years 2011–30.

Germany's labour-force growth as measured entirely reflects rising participation rates, but this is deceptive. The 15–74 age group fell a bit from 1998 until recently, reviving slightly in 2015–17. But the indigenous 15–74 population was down substantially, and it is owing to immigration that the total is only slightly down. Just from Eastern Europe (including Russia and Ukraine), Germany absorbed 1.3 million immigrants in the ten years to 2015. The salient point is that immigrants in the working-age group all arrived to work, while the indigenous 15–74s were not all 'economically active'. So the substitution of immigrants for indigenous members of the 15–74 age group raised the participation rate in the labour force.

It is little surprise that the big increase in the labour force of north-central Europe has occurred since 2010. In 2011 people from the CEE countries that joined the EU in 2004 were first allowed to take jobs in the 'old' EU. (This excludes the UK, Sweden and Ireland, which had waived 2004's seven-year moratorium on their ability to migrate.) Also the euro crisis started in 2010, and unemployment soared in Mediterranean Europe (and Ireland), particularly among youth, which is the most mobile section of the population. Youth unemployment in Greece, Italy, Spain and Portugal averaged 50% at the worst of the euro crisis. So the influx to north-central Europe was from the south as well as the east.

The growth of employment has mostly exceeded that of the labour force since 1998, especially since 2010; unemployment was relatively high in the 1990s, and again after the financial crisis. These growth rates sustained over substantial periods are unusually strong by European standards, and testify to a break with past standards, and also with past expectations.

It is an important factor in the medium-term, three-to-five-year prospects for north-central Europe that this labour force and jobs growth has come as a surprise. The OECD's 2012 forecast for the annual change in the labour force over the twenty years from 2010 could hardly show a starker contrast with current estimates of the outcome during the first seven years (one-third) of that period. The OECD's 2012 forecast for the annual change in the labour force over the twenty years from 2010 could hardly show a starker contrast with its current estimate of the outcome during the first seven years (one-third) of that period. In Germany forecasts that the labour force would be falling at ½% a year have been commonplace – the actuality of seven years growth at 1% is radically different.

Not least because demographic projections are regarded as stable, they have a big effect on investment plans. This concerns both working facilities, housing and infrastructure generally: schools, roads, electricity and other energy needs, etc.

After the severe deflation of Germany's economy in 2001–5 had knocked the stuffing out of German capex, it has not recovered – no doubt held down in part by the delusion that demographic prospects were weak, and remain so. A similar depression of investment ratios has been seen next door in Holland. But the freer, non-euro economies of Denmark, Sweden and Switzerland have seen significantly more buoyant capex, and if euro-shadowing Denmark is excluded, the ratios for Sweden and Switzerland rose above 24% of GDP in 2016.

The real growth rates of capex were initially dragged down by the 2001 slowdown, followed by Germany's extreme austerity programme. After a sharp but brief revival until 2008, the double-dip recession – financial crisis followed by euro crisis – then took its toll until 2013. A smaller recovery thereafter has been followed by real capex growth, falling back a little on the five-year moving average basis. Its average real growth is now at just over 1%, which is also the average for the whole of this century to date. As a result of this poor performance, growth of the real net capital stock has slowed sharply, accounting for much of the slowdown of productivity and potential GDP.

It is not just in directly productive capex and infrastructure that the lively build-up of labour forces and jobs should cause faster growth in future – housing too should gain, and the current emphasis of expansion, especially in Germany, is clear in construction generally, but most emphatically in housing.

While German construction activity remains far below its post-reunification level, it has taken off recently by comparison with the first ten years of this century. Both orders and output are more than 40% above the levels then and growing far faster than other elements of demand. Housing has been the strongest element in construction, but all are on an upward trend that could last for years, even if the growth rates are peaking.

This likely upswing of capex is one half of a twin process that holds out hope for a smaller structural savings glut in future. The original savings glut was an international imbalance of payments reflecting the export-led strategy of savings-glut countries. In China

Figure 35 **Savings-glut current accounts**
% of world GDP

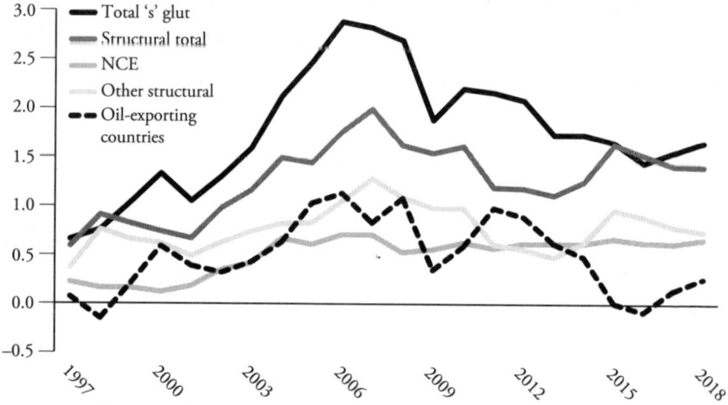

Sources: IMF, TS Lombard, author

and Japan, the savings have continued to be excessive, but both countries have since the crisis been wasting the money at home in different ways, and in China the rate of saving has also recently started to decline.

In NCE, however, the glut continues to show itself as current-account surpluses. While these are facilitated by the undervalued exchange rate, they also (by definition) represent the difference between national saving and its use in capex. This difference has been 8% of GDP in Germany, slightly less (on average) in the non-German NCE.

Mostly the current-account surplus represents the excess of private saving over capex, though governments were also in slight budget surplus. But over the next five to ten years it is likely that the capex ratios will be higher, as described above. In the paragraphs that follow we shall see that savings could well also be lower. This would squeeze the balance of payments surplus in both respects: lesser saving as well as greater capex, doubly reducing the surplus.

A major rise in the euro's FX rate should be the principal cause of this.

Personal savings rates are high in most of NCE, as they are in France, though they have been much reduced in Italy and Spain (and the UK). The effects of a shift of baby-boomers into retirement are well illustrated by late-1990s Japan. NCE has good reason for high recent personal savings rates: the generation recently passing from high late-career saving to low (or no) saving in retirement has been small, whereas the baby-boomers born after 1950 have been moving into the high-saving last part of their careers. The large baby-boomer cohort born in the 1950s and early 1960s spent 2011–16 in late career, the time of maximum saving.

As the baby-boomers pass into retirement, and shift from high to low (or no) saving, this should pull down the overall personal savings rate. At a similar phase in Japan's population growth, from the mid-1990s to the early 2000s, its personal savings rate fell to about 3–4% of disposable income from well over 10%. If the German savings rate simply halves over the next ten years, that would cut it by more than 3% of GDP. A smaller fall is likely in the non-German NCE countries. This would be a significant extra source of domestic demand in addition to the investment pressures from immigration and labour force growth discussed above.

As the extremities of Mr Draghi's ECB stimulus policies are gradually withdrawn, the incentive for NCE's $550 billion current-account inflow to be offset by flows out of Europe into higher-yielding bond markets elsewhere are reduced. Once investors see that the greater yield of, say, US Treasuries could be dwarfed by capital loss if the euro appreciates up to fair value (perhaps $1.30, perhaps more), their enthusiasm for small interest-rate gains could disappear. If so, the current-account inflows, which are similar for the EA as for the NCE, will automatically buoy the euro. Reinforcing this, good NCE economic prospects could lead to equity and real estate capital-market inflows.

This likely rise in the euro should over time erode the profitability of NCE businesses, which have been artificially favoured by the distortions arising from EA imbalances, i.e. the low relative unit labour costs in their economies. So a reduction of NCE private saving rates may not only be seen in households, but also in business saving (depreciation plus retained profits).

A further point is that fiscal discipline could be relaxed a little, with some erosion of net national savings from this quarter. The significant government budget surpluses create some room for public infrastructure spending, on top of likely higher business and housing investment.

The NCE surplus is a major source of imbalances in the world, added to surpluses in Japan and China (together about $360 billion surplus) and some Asian Tigers (another $270 billion). If NCE's surplus is added in, the total surplus of the savings-glut countries is $1.2 trillion, and NCE accounts for nearly half of it. Yet the NCE portion could fall dramatically. The total reduction of the NCE current-account surplus over five years could be at least 5% of NCE output, $400 billion (½% of world output). Together with further reduction of China's surplus, this would much reduce the deficit pressure elsewhere in the world, notably America.

Not all is rosy, however. Improved net-export performance can be expected in France and Spain, the former assuming reforms by the new government and the latter as Spain's labour-cost adjustment is now reinforcing its competitiveness. Also likely to show improved net exports are Britain, after major devaluation and with likely cuts in the consumer spending share of GDP, and Ireland, whose turnround from the euro crisis has been even more impressive than Spain's. This leaves Italy (and Greece) as potential continuing problems for the euro system.

A few years ago it seemed possible that the euro-imbalances could be resolved by faster German growth leading to overheating there and higher inflation than elsewhere. This could have reduced the divergence of labour costs with Italy, still close to fifteen percentage points. Such a development was always something of a pipe dream, given the German abhorrence of inflation.

In the event, Germany has grown fast, but has done something more interesting: it has expanded the human base of its economy by immigration and acceptance of refugees. This upsurge of labour supply has also held down wages – which is at least part of the grievance of indigenous Germans objecting to this influx of people. As already described, ordinary Germans' after-tax incomes have fallen far behind their output. Inflation has been avoided, and the economy is now short of capital. The capital stock has not kept pace with the labour input – hence the current and likely future growth of capex.

But the other aspect of this German/NCE development is that major cost divergences with Italy have not shrunk. There are two conceptual solutions to this problem, and various non-solutions that would constitute 'muddling through' or 'kicking the can down the road'. The two solutions are either that Italy (also Greece) leaves the euro; or the EA adopts a fiscal union involving much greater assistance of weaker elements by the stronger elements – whether such elements are countries, regions, people or whatever.

The problem with the solutions is that each provokes strong opposition. Nearly 60% of Italians, for example, want to stay in the EA – even though their experience under it has been disastrous and this disaster has been made much worse by the euro system itself. Greeks are similar. Italians may dislike what has happened to them since 1999, but they have in the past argued that rule from Brussels is preferable to rule from Rome. And the methods of EA governance mean that they will not be pushed out of the euro if and when they are in trouble – they will simply be forced to fend for themselves within the euro, with minimal help from EA 'partners'.

When it comes to a fiscal union, the obstacle is (unsurprisingly) the likely payers, though not just them. September 2017's German elections saw the centrist parties of the Grand Coalition

– the centre-right Christian Democrats (CDU, also the Christian Social Union, CSU, in Bavaria) and the centre-left Social Democrats (SPD) – lose about fourteen percentage points of their votes. The far left and Greens gained a little, but the chief gains were by the Free Democrats (centre-right liberals) and the *Alternative für Deutschland* (AfD), a party that started a few years ago as an academically inspired anti-euro party but changed after the 2015 influx of refugees to an anti-foreigner party. For all the SPD's advocacy of a fiscal union in the EA, and its membership of the now much weakened Grand Coalition, Germany will not actually permit it to happen, as it would slash the CDU/CSU vote further.

Aside from Germany's natural reservations about fiscal union, as one of the largest potential payers to poorer areas, the same view is held by the Dutch, who also have a veto on any such arrangement – with a constitutional provision for a referendum that can be triggered by citizens, not just the government. Both Germany and Holland are in any case confronted with potentially increased net payments into the EU budget, now that Britain is leaving.

Spain is likely to be equally intransigent, however. Having borne enormous social and economic costs over 2008–15 to become competitive within the euro, Spain could be very unsympathetic to countries that duck the painful reforms needed to match its performance. So the chances of an effective EA fiscal union are small.

This issue could come to a head in 2019 or 2020. As of now the EA is competitive on costs – with strong growth of world trade, exports are growing fast. Yet the starting point is that the 2017 current-account surplus was already $440 billion. If Danish, Swedish and Swiss surpluses are added to this the total is $550 billion, including the whole of NCE. The domestic economies are also running hot, with strong consumer spending and capex, while governments are intending an extra dollop of fiscal stimulus in Germany, Italy, France and Spain.

If the ECB tries to stay excessively easy to resist euro appreciation the economy will overheat very quickly, ensuring the currency appreciates. But if it reduces its current extreme stimulus the euro will certainly go up. So the euro should appreciate whatever the ECB wants or does – it has lost control of the rate, just like the Bank of Japan from mid-2015.

As the euro goes up, ultra-rapid German growth could fall back a bit, and Italy would suffer both from lesser exports to Germany and weakened competitiveness in the rest of the world. Possibly, renewed crisis will provoke Italy to the kind of market-friendly reforms it has so far refused, at painful cost. But it seems unlikely.

15

Will Britain muddle through Brexit?

While France and Italy have had renegade parties for years, and Greece elected one that turned out to be bluffers, the June 2016 Brexit vote was the first indication that centrist politicians had better take neo-Luddism seriously. This author abstained in the Brexit referendum. Why? For three reasons that underpin the analysis below:

- At a simple level, my heart said Remain, my head said Leave.
- Economically, the long-run consequences seem unlikely to be large.
- The campaigns on both sides were exaggerated and obnoxious.

There were and are strong arguments on both sides. These affect Britain's economic prospects after the presumed consummation of Brexit in March 2019, and subsequently through whatever transitional arrangements are made with the EU.

Summary arguments for Remain:

- 'If it works, don't fix it' – Britain's economy has outperformed continental countries for the past thirty-five years, not chiefly because of EU membership, but certainly with that as context.
- Further to this, interim uncertainty between the June 2016 vote and actual exit hurts the economy, and also, especially, the

position of EU citizens in Britain and British citizens living elsewhere in the EU.

- Free movement of labour is a good principle, inherently better than restricted movement, with economic benefits that will cause costs in the course of the transition out of the EU.
- The UK will have to duplicate several functions, e.g. trade policy, normally performed by the EU, both wastefully and potentially suffering from a shortage of relevant skills.
- Britain's demonstrated comparative advantage in finance and professional services argues against a change that will shift some such functions out of London.
- Brexit poses some risks to peaceful development in Ireland on either side of the border, whose status was laid down in 1998's Good Friday Agreement.
- Whatever the merits and demerits of nationalism, a unified European polity may be helpful in coping with future dealings with Russia, the US, China, etc.

Summary arguments for Brexit:

- The bulk of the EU, or at least its ruling class, is or claims to be clearly set on a course towards some form of pan-European state that the British equally clearly do not want.
- Resulting from this, the eurozone is the real future form of the EU, and Britain's enviable non-membership of it implies gradual separation that should be welcome. The euro is a failed project, ill conceived to start with, brutal in its enforcement since 2009, and extremely damaging to the rest of the world, particularly the EA's largest trading partner, Britain.
- Similarly, Britain is not in the Schengen system of supposedly passport-free movement, which is weakening under the weight of various countries' understandable objections.
- Relatively undemocratic policy formation in the EU has been

altered under the pressure of the euro crisis to permit changes that should require treaty change to be pushed through by means of qualified majority voting – the extent to which this will be employed in other matters is unclear and potentially removes British national prerogatives.

- England (not Britain), by 2015 more densely populated than Holland, has the densest population of any sizeable country in Europe (i.e. excluding Gibraltar, Malta, etc.), and immigration has made this population increase rapidly, concentrated in the already overcrowded south-east.
- For thirty years problems in British society, instead of being tackled, have been sidestepped by importing cheap foreign labour, rather than investment in training, equipment to raise productivity and wages, programmes to reduce social divisions, and so forth.
- Low-income immigration has hurt the wages of low-paid people, and studies said to minimise this effect are inapplicable owing to their restrictive assumptions.
- English nationalism is a natural response to the fact that for several decades England has subsidised Scotland, Wales and Northern Ireland, as well as the EU budget – it is a force to be reckoned with, not sneered at.
- A return to agricultural policies similar to those in place before Britain joined the EU in 1973 would lower food prices substantially, as the EU's Common Agricultural Policy inflates food prices by as much as 20%, hurting poorer people most.

The Brexit vote was close, at 52–48 for Leave versus Remain. The broad breakdown was that English industrial regions and Wales preferred Leave, while London and much of the prosperous south-east, together with Scotland and Northern Ireland, preferred Remain. Within England, this roughly reflects the interests of the various parts of the country, and also the protest votes of economic losers versus winners. The Northern Irish attitude was protective of 1998's Good Friday 'peace deal' between the six counties and the Republic. Scotland has been a country of emigration for at least three centuries, and has no interest in restraining free movement of labour, either in or out.

That the vote went the way it did – it would only have taken a modest number of people voting the other way for the result to have been reversed – reflects the effects of the eurozone's failures, and of the damaging effects of 2010–16's British Chancellor of the Exchequer, George Osborne.

Before looking at the economic environment at the time of the vote, however, the immigration numbers are important. The Leave campaign pitched its appeal to those objecting to the huge flow of immigration. In the decades before 2000, the growth rate of the UK labour force was 0.3% a year. Since then it has been 0.8%, ½% a year higher. This difference is more than fully accounted for by immigration, given the slowing of the indigenous population.

Britain's relatively liberal jobs market, in contrast to heavily regulated continental regimes, meant people who managed to get into the country could get work, in many cases at a significant premium to what they might have earned in their country of origin. Migrants making it only to France, for example, seemed either unable to have a chance of employment there, or keener in any case to get to Britain – even to the point of holing themselves up in the notorious 'Sangatte' camps near Calais (in its role as a northern extremity of the Schengen system). They have since been dispersed by the French authorities in a fashion that would probably not be legal in the UK.

In 2004, the EU was extended to the east, to include Poland, the Czech Republic, Slovakia, Hungary, Slovenia and 'the Balts' (Lithuania, Latvia and Estonia). In 2007, they were joined by Bulgaria and Romania. In each case, inhabitants of these countries were subject to a seven-year moratorium on migration to work in the 'old EU', i.e. all of Western Europe but Switzerland and Norway. This moratorium was waived, however, by Sweden, Ireland and Britain.

Ironically, the countries most determined to prevent Britain having restraints on EU-sourced immigration in 2015–16's attempted renegotiation by then UK Prime Minister Cameron of free movement of labour were those anxious to keep the east-bloc people out a few years earlier, i.e. Germany and France. And Britain, a model devotee of free markets under Labour Prime Minister Blair in 2004 and 2007, found that a lot of its citizens were not so keen on the resultant migrant inflow.

Immigration to Britain in the 1990s ran at a gross 250,000–280,000 a year, but was nearly matched by gross emigration, so that net immigration was trivial, averaging well under 50,000 a year until 1997. In 1998–2003, encouraged by the Labour government that came to power in mid-1997, the gross annual number jumped toward 500,000, and the net number to 140,000–180,000. In 2004, the admission of the former east-bloc countries saw the gross immigrant numbers rise again to just under 600,000, and the net number to an average in 2004–15 of about 275,000. A sharp increase latterly reflected the euro crisis, adding southern European youth to the east-bloc migrants (driven by 50% average youth unemployment in Greece, Italy, Spain and Portugal).

Considering the seven-year moratoria on east-bloc migration had expired for all but Bulgaria and Romania by 2011, and the latter two in 2014, this continued move to the UK is a tribute to the disaster that the euro had imposed on its members – and indeed on neighbours such as the UK, as well as countries further afield.

The Remain campaign had little to offer against the obvious economic reality that increased supply depresses the price – of any commodity, not just labour – except studies purporting to show that the effect was small, and confined to low-income jobs. A much-cited example was a paper in 2015 by Sir Stephen Nickell and Jumana Saleheen of Oxford University for the Bank of England, where

Nickell had previously served on the Monetary Policy Committee. While this presents a sophisticated analysis of the short-term impact of migration, it has little relevance for the question of whether large-scale, prolonged migration lowers wages.

In page 2 of the Nickell–Saleheen paper a footnote observes – of a US study of migration effects also showing only a small impact on low-skilled wages – 'This would appear to be at variance with standard economics based on supply and demand. The most convincing explanation is that there is a weaker adoption of advanced technology, which is complementary to skilled labour, in the presence of larger numbers of the unskilled.' In other words, the studies do not take account of the natural tendency of employers, confronted with readily available cheap labour, to use it rather than take the risk involved in labour-substitution capex, on technology and labour-saving equipment, training for higher skills, etc. – the absence of all of which tends to hold down real wages in the longer term.

Economically, socially and politically, probably the strongest argument for Brexit is the point made initially: 'For thirty years problems in British society, instead of being tackled, have been side-stepped by importing cheap foreign labour, rather than investment in training, equipment to raise productivity and wages, programmes to reduce social divisions, and so forth'.

This tendency has been seen under Conservative and Labour governments, and goes back to the aftermath of the coal miners' strike that was defeated in 1985. The defeat of the miners was necessary, but divisive. The failure of policy arose *after* the miners' defeat. It should have been followed by a major reconciliation programme to integrate the industrial Midlands, Wales and the North into the new, market-orientated British economy.

In fact, however, the mining regions were left to 'stew in their own juice', nursing resentments against a triumphalist Conservative government, and falling back on the social security system for sustenance: generations of people living on welfare, with little or no work ethic. Jobs that should have been made more valuable by training and investment have instead been done by low-wage foreigners.

Over the years there can be little doubt that absence of proper investment and social systems has undermined low-skilled wage levels. It takes no imagination to see that a partially sullen indigenous population confronted with foreign workers ready to do menial jobs at below living wages will generate resentment. In a densely populated and long-standing country like England, this naturally has led to trouble, including, finally, voter revolt – neo-Luddism.

Of course, if recent immigrants are willing to be nurses for low wages, it is tempting not to spend money training indigenous citizens to be nurses, especially as they will also expect higher wages. And if foreigners will work at low wages to pick crops on farms in brutal conditions imposed by 'gangmasters', nobody will develop robots to do so, even though they could.

Farmers, ironically, mostly voted for Brexit. Yet the best free-market case for the economy under Brexit has been presented by Professor Patrick Minford of Cardiff, and the chief benefits to the British economy in his analysis arise because of lower food and land prices. Granted, the latter refers chiefly to non-agricultural land – fortunately for his analysis, since the chief driver of high land prices in the countryside is not the EU's agricultural policy but the exemption from death duties of agricultural land.

The benefit of lower food prices will require withdrawal of subsidies under the EU's common agricultural policy from all but the hardest-pressed farmers, as food will mostly be imported from cheaper sources than current over-subsidised EU farmers. This policy nettle has yet to be grasped by the post-Brexit-vote Conservative government, which draws a lot of political support from the farming community. The convulsions of the post-Brexit British policy could resemble those of the mid-1840s, with the adoption of free trade and the abolition of the Corn Laws, destroying the government of the day.

Apart from Minford and his pro-Brexit colleagues, the Leave case was proposed largely on the assumed ability to enjoy the end of Britain's net contributions to the EU budget of some £10 billion a year, about ½% of total output. Various claims have been made about how this might be spent, but the political realities of the transition after official EU exit in March 2019 mean that this benefit may not be felt for many years.

Unsurprisingly, countries like Germany and Holland that make major contributions to the EU budget are distressed by the potential loss of Britain's. For all their interest in good future trading links with the UK, they are just as keen as the more emotional EU elements to keep the cash flowing out of the UK for as long as possible under transitional arrangements for which the UK seems willing to pay a substantial fee.

The intellectual opposition to the Minford position is even weaker, consisting largely of a Treasury pre-Brexit-vote paper of extraordinary bias, backed up by half-baked material from the London School of Economics suggesting that British trade with the EU might fall by 60%, despite the common external EU tariff being between 3% and 4%.

The Treasury produced a forecast suggesting that over fifteen years Britain would lose about 1% of real income growth a year, including immediate recession after Brexit. This latter has been confounded by on-trend growth since mid-2016 despite the enforced start of a badly needed rebalancing from the distortions of the economy over the past fifteen years, and especially ill-judged policies in the post-crisis recovery since 2009.

Britain has an open economy, in which exports and imports have much increased their share of total output over the past ten years, from about 25% to about 30%, counting goods and services. The share of the EA in exports has been falling, but only relative to a growing importance of trade in the economy; so it has remained about 13% of total output. The euro crisis damaged this significant element of total demand. Additionally, it added continental money to the already huge flow of funds into the UK, mostly to London and its environs, from such places as Russia, the Middle East, China and elsewhere in the Far East.

With collapse of oil prices in late 2014 and the simultaneous adoption of predatory devaluation by the EA that was already in large overseas surplus, the flow of cash from the EA became more important, even though OPEC and the former Soviet Union had less cash. The pound's real exchange rate rose sharply, and became significantly less competitive. This added to the difficulties of Britain's industrial areas, already acute enough after the EA's double-dip recession. And the impact of the euro crisis was immediately evident in the surge of immigrants from Mediterranean Europe. So in industrial areas business had to cope with weak demand and higher relative costs, while labour saw its income undermined by desperate immigrants.

Added to the aggravations of the euro crisis has been the 2010–16 rhetoric and performance of the UK government, notably George Osborne, Chancellor of the Exchequer. The Conservative-led coalition with the Liberal Democrats after the 2010 election enabled Osborne to blame the financial crisis on the previous Labour government, and he compounded this by announcing tremendous budgetary rigour as the price of Labour's failure. In reality, the cuts were not fierce in current spending – investment bore the brunt. Then in 2014–15 the economy was reviving from the rigours of recession and the euro crisis, so that some pull-back of the budget deficit would have been timely. But Osborne relaxed the austerity programme in the interests of winning the 2015 election.

Osborne's policy was poor in at least three ways. First, he hit the economy hardest when it was already weakest because of the financial crisis, and then eased up on austerity just when the economy could have borne some fiscal tightening, given recovery: a classic case of policy designed to suit party, rather than national, interests.

Second, his toughest austerity came when the euro crisis was at its worst, and was already thwarting British recovery; he failed to understand the world economy.

Lastly, the focus on cuts in investment was particularly ill advised at a time when UK (and world) interest rates – especially those for government debt – were well below inflation. Badly needed infrastructure could have been built at negative real cost, helping to spur recovery. Government capex, adjusted for inflation, fell 5.4% in 2011, 7.2% in 2012 and 3.5% in 2013. In the pre-election year of 2014, with the EA and UK already in significant recovery, it was boosted by 8.6%.

Possibly as significant as Osborne's actual policy was his (largely false) rhetoric of austerity that earned him widespread dislike. When it came to the Brexit vote in 2016, his aggressive advocacy of the Remain position, together with his clear misunderstanding of how the euro crisis had undermined his own policies, was compounded by absurd and obviously biased UK Treasury forecasts of both immediate and long-term economic disaster should people vote Leave.

Osborne further undermined the Remain position by saying he would have to impose major budgetary austerity if the Leave position were to win. When it did, perhaps partly as a protest against him, he promptly reversed that position. So did the Governor of the Bank of England, who had unwisely been almost as outspoken. Coming on top of obviously biased forecasts, it is arguable that this kind of misrepresentation is worse when done by the Chancellor of the Exchequer from the Treasury, one of the great departments of state, than the similarly exaggerated, wilder claims of dissident, pro-Brexit leaders.

The British economy had shifted under Osborne's pre-election stimulus policies into the unsustainable position of locomotive, dragging along the (much bigger) European economy, with the pound's real exchange rate too high and the euro's too low. The Brexit vote therefore accelerated badly needed adjustment. Financial markets believed the prophets of doom and the pound fell sharply. After a few months in which consumers cut their savings rate to offset the rise of import prices entailed by devaluation, its toll has slowed consumer spending.

Rebalancing of an economy generally involves a slowdown, and in Britain's case the current-account deficit, 6% of output in the first half of 2016, has begun to be reduced by newly cost-competitive exports; but rebalancing and growth are hindered by inhibition of business capex owing to Brexit-related uncertainties. In Britain's favour has been good growth of world trade, and the relatively strong advance of the continental European economy, motivated for the first time since German reunification to a great degree by domestic demand.

Over the longer term, a reasonable settlement of free trade between Britain and the EU is likely, despite the ups and downs of current negotiations. The British are clearly keen. The EU negotiating position seems obdurate at times, but the huge continental surplus in its trade with Britain makes it the potential loser from cuts in trade. This raises the obvious question: 'How many thousands of German workers (for example, and it would be many thousands) would the German government really be prepared to see lost just to teach the British a lesson?' The answer is at most 'not many', more likely 'none'.

Some high-value financial jobs in London will be lost to the continent, though financial market restrictions in Paris and Frankfurt may well drive people back to London quite quickly. The tendency towards financial controls and meddling on the continent are chief reasons the markets have until now grown so fast in London. Equally, some shift of business in Britain away from finance and professional services to industry and exports should rebalance incomes both away from the south-east in favour of the Midlands, the North and Wales; and towards low-wage earners as competition from cheap foreign labour is reduced, a lower real exchange rate helps industrial areas and productivity-enhancing capex increases.

The reduction of immigration certainly implies a slower growth rate for total British output. Increased labour input has been a major source of growth this century; slower labour-force growth is highly likely to reduce overall potential growth. For example, as shown in the previous chapter, in the nineteen years of the euro, 1999–2017, real output per head in Germany and Britain has grown by about the same amount (26–7%). But in Britain immigration has raised the population so that total output has risen 41%; in Germany immigration has merely offset the decline of the indigenous German population so that total output has risen by 26%, the same as output per head. In future, total output growth in Britain should be lower.

Whether British output per head will be lower in future is much less clear, for all the UK Treasury's dire forecasts. Some cut in high-income financial work would reduce average incomes. But less downward pressure on low wages from immigration implies the opposite. Clearly, the distribution of income is likely to become less unequal, both as between rich and poor; between London/south-east and more industrial regions; and as a result of cheaper food. So far this point has not been picked up by the 'commentariat', which is generally opposed to Brexit.

16

Euro-populism – to worsen or to cure global imbalances?

An ironic aspect of the British debate about Brexit has been that not only are Brexit's chief proponents largely provincial in outlook – so are those wishing to remain in the EU! The habit of being rude about leaders, and politicians in general, is deeply ingrained in Britain, so each side tends to rant about the defects of the other's argument. But it is what is happening on the continent that is much more important, for Europe obviously, perhaps also Britain, but certainly the wider world.

A trade war initiated by President Trump is a major threat to growth, both in potentially weakening or ending this promising medium-term cyclical upswing, and for the long term. For all Trump's frivolous talk about 'winning' a trade war, the reality of such a war would at best be a case of who is least damaged – without any country actually gaining. As discussed in the next chapter, the current disputes between the US and China are likely to be settled as part of a multifaceted negotiation. But in the economic downswing likely in late 2019 or 2020, the US could (quite rightly) focus on its global deficit – which is chiefly vis-à-vis Europe – rather than its bilateral deficit, which is largest with China.

In all probability the US would be less damaged than Europe in a trade war for the simple reason that it has a trade deficit – its imports exceed its exports, so that shrinkage of both would not necessarily cut domestic demand. In continental Europe the savings-glut NCE would be hard pressed to generate domestic demand to substitute for the loss of its net export surplus.

The sad point is that, whatever one's views about Trump personally, the point he makes about the predatory policies of Japan and the NCE is correct. Savings-glut countries have for decades now been pursuing undervalued currencies and net export surpluses that have depended for their existence and continuance on the willingness of the US to run the corresponding deficits. These US (and other countries') deficits have tended to be matched by a run-up of domestic debt. They have also worsened America's net balance of international assets and liabilities.

Trump is probably wrong to suppose that the US economy as a whole is seriously worse off as a result of these predatory savings-glut exchange-rate policies. Possession of a somewhat overvalued exchange rate is far from obviously a disadvantage, even over the long term. It tends to force firms to hold costs down, raising productivity, and to siphon capital and labour toward high-value activities as low-value businesses yield to foreign competition.

But that is, of course, the issue: it is employees in the lower-value businesses that have suffered from the dollar overvaluation that is the flip side of the undervalued yen and euro (and, until about 2011, the Chinese yuan). And the people in lower-valued businesses in America are the Trump voters.

In effect, the savings-glut countries' pursuit of undervaluation, by adding to the travails of America's losers, the swing-voters for Trump, have enabled the divisions within US society to yield a US president ready to play chicken over world trade. So the imbalances within the eurozone are not just an issue for the countries involved. German and Italian unit labour costs have stayed 15% or more out of line with one another for a dozen years. The ECB's determination to set an exchange rate that supports hobbled Italy ensures a massive continental European surplus, as Germany is in consequence more than 10% undervalued vis-à-vis its own long-run relative cost position, and has been now for twelve years.

The EA surplus, which together with non-EA countries (Switzerland, Sweden and Denmark) is approaching $600 billion, imposes real-income losses on lower-income Americans, whose interests Trump represents, even if the US economy as a whole is not made worse off. Of course, Japan is also part of the problem. But even though its surplus of about $195 billion, at 4% of output, slightly exceeds the EA ratio, it is under 1% of total US output, versus the continental European 3%. Trump's electoral chances in 2020 depend on the perception of Midwestern manufacturing employees as to whether he has successfully defended them from predatory trading practices. His trade war is only superficially with China – it is in reality with Europe, and within Europe the NCE, and within the NCE, Germany.

But populist reactions to globalisation and technology are not confined to the US Midwest. They are widespread in Europe too, with the Brexit vote simply the most conspicuous case, as well as the first major governmental consequence of it. Nor is populism the dirty word that many continental politicians in the traditional ruling parties make it out to be. Progress certainly should not be at the pace of the slowest – but neither should it be at the pace of the fastest. Respect is due to society's losers as well as its winners. That is the economics of populism.

The originator of the word 'meritocracy' was Michael Young, a British Labour politician, who coined it in 1958. He saw it as a dystopia, not a utopia. He feared a society divided in almost Darwinian fashion into hereditary winners and losers. Has that vision proved accurate?

As observed at the start of this book, the neo-Luddites have the vote. For believers in democracy therefore, it is crucial to ensure that recognition of merit, and rewards according to it, do not create a dystopia. There is very little sign that this has been understood, let alone accepted, amongst the EU (or even the British or American) elite. They see demagogue politicians taking advantage of popular discontent as barbarians at the gate – to be fought off by whatever means are available, which often means adoption of the demagogues' policies.

The arguments outlined above (Chapter 14) concerning internal EA imbalances in 2019–20 do not hold out much hope for a satisfactory resolution of them. Equally unlikely is either of the two actual solutions for the imbalances: Italian (and presumably Greek) exit from the euro, or adoption of a fiscal union that would entail long-term acceptance of such differences in competitiveness, along the lines of the long-run divergence between, for example, New England and the Deep South in the US.

But with or without either of these solutions, the euro is likely to mount much higher, reflecting the massive surpluses. Italian euro exit, were it actually to occur, would give the euro an extra fillip, of course, as it would remove the EA country most responsible for holding it down (via higher relative costs) and would also suggest less need for ultra-easy monetary policy. But even with Italy still in, the euro could continue to appreciate strongly.

Current ECB projections for the EA economy unambiguously suggest overheating, which will be a factor pulling up the euro. The expected growth rate is above potential through 2020, implying that overheating increases. But the rising euro could hold down inflation (via cheaper imports), giving the ECB 'doves' the excuse they seek to return only very slowly to more normal interest rates. This suggests that a rising nominal as well as real exchange rate will be the chief means by which the EA economy is brought back to its longer-run trend of output.

As inflationary pressures are already in evidence, and 2018–20 growth could be above-potential by well over 1% in aggregate, eventual cooling off of the implied overheating could require close to zero growth for more than a year early in the 2020s. The increase in the real exchange rate could be caused in part by inflation exceeding expectations, but the bulk of the effect is likely to be in the nominal rate, probably including a dollar rate for the euro soaring well over $1.30 at some stage – i.e. becoming 5% overvalued as opposed to 5% undervalued now.

The starting point for policy in EA countries is the 2017–18 election cycle in Holland, France, Germany and Italy, which followed closely on the Brexit vote of mid-2016. In Holland the long-established, anti-immigration/euro Freedom Party lost ground, raising hopes among mainstream EA politicians. In France, however, in round one of the presidential election, half the votes went to dissident candidates, with the rightist National Front a little behind the combined renegade Socialist candidates. French politics then lurched back to a constructive channel with the success of President Macron and his new party.

The German election saw a major setback for the centrist, 'grand' coalition of the CDU/CSU (Christian Democrats) and the SPD (Social Democrats). The CDU/CSU moved from 42% to 33% of the vote, and the SPD fell from 26% to 21%. Votes for the rightist anti-immigration/euro 'Alternative for Germany' (AfD) rose to 12½% from 2013's 4¾%, and for the Free Democratic Party (economic liberals) to 10¾% from 4¾% (in both cases entering the Bundestag, as their below-5% share in 2013 was just below the 5% threshold). The Grand Coalition has been re-formed, with difficulty. As polls suggested that a rerun of the vote would put the SPD behind the AfD, the SPD dropped its promise not to return to the coalition. But the open-door policy towards immigrants and refugees has been effectively repudiated by the electorate.

Equally importantly for the next few years, the question of a budgetary union has been put in play. This is already strongly proposed and favoured by Macron – and obviously by its natural beneficiaries such as Italy. Mediterranean Europe already dreads the combination of needed normalisation of monetary policy with the choice of a successor to Draghi as ECB head (from October 2019).

Any successor is likely to be more hawkish on policy. Though the ECB has in reality already lost control of the euro's exchange rate – the true target of its policy – it is not yet fully aware of that, and wants current ultra-easy interest rates to last as long as possible. Germany will want to take the top ECB job: it has so far been held by a Dutchman, a Frenchman and an Italian. The new deputy head being Spanish rules out a Spaniard.

The strategy of the Mediterranean group (including France) is to create objections to the current Bundesbank President, Jens Weidmann, as being too hawkish and having been too contentious in his role as Germany's person on the ECB Council. One goal might have been to get German concessions on the budgetary union in exchange for accepting Weidmann or another German as ECB President. The problem for the German coalition is that the autumn 2021 election is likely to come at a weak point in the economic cycle. A move to budgetary union by then could boost even further the AfD vote, and probably also the ex-Communist leftists, at the expense of the centrist parties. As the new SPD Finance Minister is a lot less keen on EA fiscal union than his party, CDU/CSU objections have already more or less destroyed Macron's hopes for fiscal union.

Meanwhile, Italian politics has thrown up as tricky a situation as Germany's. The March 2018 election made the essentially anarchist, and clearly anti-establishment Five-Star Movement (M5S) the largest party, with over 32% of the vote. The Northern League separatist party got 17.7% and a new rightist party, 'Brothers of Italy', 4.4%, so that dissident parties had a total well over 50%. 'Forza Italia', the centre-right party under former Prime Minister Berlusconi, only took 14% of the vote, while the previously ruling Democratic Party got only 19%. This was a sound beating for the traditional, centrist parties that have ruled Italy since World War II, though of course the entire system had already been up-ended by 'Tangentopoli' in the mid-1990s.

Like any other country, Italy can get along without a government for a while. But it seems clear that the Italian electorate is kicking over the traces. Yet the economics of the almost inevitable cyclical downturn in the EA economies in 2020 are likely to make an already parlous situation worse. And in Germany, if the population finds itself shoehorned by the machinations of EA politics into subsidy for Italy (and other poor relations), with continued influx of foreigners holding down indigenous Germans' wage incomes, the political dangers are equally acute.

It is possible to imagine benign results from the kind of scenario painted here. For example, If Italians finally came to understand what a disaster euro membership has been for them and voted in politicians committed to euro-exit, that would be a positive outcome for Italy, the EA and the world.

An alternative benign result would be if German voters were to respond to Germany's relatively benign prospects and economic performance by gradual, if probably grudging, acceptance of the costs to them of fiscal union. But is this less unlikely than Italian acceptance of the desirability of euro-exit? It would accord with the standard strategy of advocates of a European superstate: mission creep towards full union. But such a resolution of the potential EA tensions of 2020–21 is less likely than voters' rejection of a drift towards fiscal union for three reasons:

1. German voters' shift against the centrist parties is only partly a reflection of households' after-tax incomes having fallen 10% behind the economy's output over the nineteen years of the euro. It also reflects Germany having avoided inflation and population shrinkage by means of major immigration, and acceptance of refugees. The coherent culture of the post-World War II German democracy has not easily accepted outright foreigners, as was seen from the 1950s onward in the treatment of Turkish guest workers. In any solution of EA imbalances by means of cross-subsidy, the continued cost advantages of Germany versus EA

partners would continue to suck in labour, with the dilution of German 'identity' that has been marked since 2010. This will enhance the appeal of the AfD and the extreme left.

2. Similar considerations apply to Holland, where the economy has been even less successful than Germany's in rewarding ordinary workers, and anti-immigrant politics is longer established.
3. Spain will need palliating for any major cross-subsidies to be possible. After the pain of its post-crisis adjustment, Spain will probably only accept an easier deal for Italy if it also revives the pre-2008 tendency of the EU budget to spend large amounts in Spain. But such an arrangement would add to the burden on Germany and Holland at a time when they no longer have the UK alongside them as major net revenue contributor.

This chapter's heading asked whether euro-populism is likely to worsen or to cure global imbalances. The answer is that a sharp increase of Italian political dissidence – presumably under the pressure of and early 2020s recession – could be a cure, if it finally provokes Italian exit from the euro. But German populism is likely to operate against fiscal union, the only other resolution of eurozone imbalances. And at present, German populism seems more focused than the Italian variety. As regards the EA budget it is defending the status quo, not proposing change.

The sad consequence of these points, in the context of the forces that have given rise to the Trump Presidency – and which seem likely to increase rather than diminish over time – is that the current, promising world economic advance has a substantial chance of being cut off by a breakdown of globalisation. A world slowdown is highly likely within two to three years; in response to that defensive policy action could well include seriously protectionist measures.

17

Summary: Can/should the tide of populism be turned?

So far we have seen that growth has been re-established on an adequate scale in the advanced countries and China, with reasonably good medium-term prospects. This view depends on the analysis suggesting hi-tech benefits to the US economy and consumer welfare are significantly under-measured in the official growth data. The downsides are resumption of Japanese weakness, potential trouble in Italy and Greece from a likely major appreciation of the euro, and likely continued rising inequality from hi-tech in particular, with globalisation fading as its source.

While medium-term economic prospects seem benign, the US and EA economies are both growing at above-potential rates, with rising inflation. The means by which this upward cycle in these economies may end is also becoming clear. The EA is much more sensitive to the exchange rate than to interest rates directly. But the use of monetary ease to hold down the euro has suffered diminishing returns – to the point where the European Central Bank (ECB) has lost control of the euro's FX rate, like the Bank of Japan before it with the yen. Under any scenario of ECB policy, the euro should rise substantially, slowing the German economy and probably putting Italy into recession. (If the ECB stays ultra-easy to protect Italy, the EA will overheat and the euro appreciate; but if the ECB becomes less loose, the euro goes up anyhow.)

Figure 36 **Real FX rates**
Producer-price basis, long-run average = 100

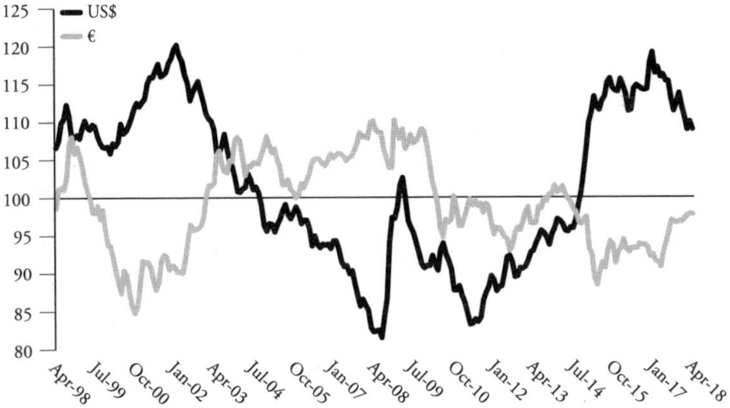

Sources: JP Morgan, Datastream, TS Lombard, author

The American economy, more classical than the EA, is directly sensitive to interest rates more than to the dollar. But the dollar, as well as being weak against the yen and euro, is also weak against the Chinese yuan and Canadian dollar, and even possibly against the Mexican peso, these five being its major trading partners. Given the large surpluses that have spilled into US financial markets from Japan and the EA, dollar weakness could reduce the downward pressure on US bond yields from this source. Yet as well as the upward pressure on rates and yields from rapid growth, the US has a budget deficit swollen by fresh tax cuts and by the Federal Reserve deciding to sell some of its holdings of US government debt. As foreigners' downward pressure on US interest rates lessens, the upside for them probably exceeds current financial market expectations.

A big question is, when do the US rates/yields pass over the threshold from 'strong economy drives up rates' to 'high rates cause economy to slow'? The answer is likely to be when US government bond yields approach 4%, perhaps sometime in the middle of 2019, when short-term US interest rates could be in the 3% region. The economy would then grow more slowly in 2020, a US presidential election year. The timetable for euro strength causing a renewed bout of euro-imbalance problems – aka Italian recession – is about the same. Japan's tag-along, export-dependent economy could hit trouble as soon as the rest of the world ceases to provide the growth on which it depends.

A sense of trouble to come has been provided by President Trump's willingness to risk US self-harm by means of import restrictions against China. The resolution of this involves three other relevant factors:

- US anxiety about loss of its hegemon status in a world moving from unipolar (post-Cold War) to multipolar, as China, in particular, becomes a larger economy than the US and increasingly willing to use its strength
- US grievances about supposedly illicit technology transfer to Chinese firms
- North Korea.

China had used North Korea as a bargaining chip for a long time. Every time it engaged in particularly aggressive moves, US officials would head for Beijing asking the Chinese to get Pyongyang under control. The Chinese would be polite, ask for whatever they wanted in return, and essentially do nothing. The big change now has been the willingness of the US to engage in trade restrictions causing self-harm alongside substantially greater harm to China and other net exporters. This has changed the calculus in favour of restraining North Korea – with possibly dramatic results in terms of North–South peace and nuclear disarmament.

By delivering President Trump a major North Korean 'win', and making some (probably token) concessions on trade and 'intellectual property', China is able to secure:

- the end of import restrictions that in any case raised major domestic hostility in America (leaving aside US people likely to be damaged by Chinese and other countries' retaliation)
- shelving for now of US concerns about no longer being global No. 1.

The 'who is No. 1 issue' is unlikely to go away, however. And neither will the issue of US overseas deficits and the predatory exchange-rate behaviour engaged in by savings-glut countries to secure the corresponding surpluses. The former means Sino–US tensions are virtually certain for the indefinite future. The latter, however, switches focus to Europe and Japan, now that China's surplus is minimal and its excessive saving and capex receding (if only gradually).

In theory, Germany's likely shrinkage of its huge savings surplus over investment, together with a big rise in the euro, should slash the EA surplus. Meanwhile, Japan is an ever less important part of the world economy, so its surpluses could cease to be a major concern.

But there are two euro-issues: timing and Italy. Germany's shift away from its current major domestic imbalances could take ten years – but the next US downswing is likely within two. And even with German rebalancing and a major euro appreciation, Germany would probably still end up with a surplus and Italy a deficit. On the way, Italy would have had a recession, with consequences for the whole EA, and therefore the world economy.

Meanwhile, the US trade hawks are fully aware that measures based on bilateral trade imbalances – as between the US and China – are essentially fallacious. The overall US deficit has its global counterpart in continental Europe and Japan. If a US economic downswing starts just in time for the 2020 election year, the attack could switch from China to Europe. And intellectually the US trade hawks will have the better of the argument, for all the benefits of free trade. The reality is that damage caused by the eurozone's troubles has been global, not just a local or regional problem.

In considering the measures needed to minimise damage from these threats, and from justified aspects of populism, we must remember the optimal approach discussed in Chapter 1 of this book:

- Pursuit of maximum growth requires compensation to losers from the changes that growth requires.
- Increasingly, losers are going to be displaced by tech, not globalisation.
- But political realities are that when in trouble people tend to blame foreigners, even when their problems are mostly home-made.

The 'should' in the title to this chapter reflects the fact that populism has its roots in popular distress arising from economic failures and developments: financial crisis and poor recovery, hi-tech destruction of lower-middle-income jobs, dangerous and damaging overambition and incompetence in the form and conduct of the euro area, and so forth. Popular resentment of such things through the ballot box should be a source of pride in democracy, not something to deplore. What can be deplorable (a loaded word after the US 2016 elections) is demagogues taking advantage of justified popular resentments. But even then the demagogues are frequently making just criticisms of prevailing systems and/or rulers. It is essential to listen – even to demagogues – rather than to dismiss them out of hand, as either malignant or stupid, or both.

Democracy in England originated in the trade-off between the king and the people. The king wanted money (through taxation), notably to fight wars. The people, through Parliament, insisted on redress of grievances as a condition of voting in the taxes. Redress of grievances should today be the goal in dealing with populism.

A helpful factor, described above, is that the key developed-world economies, especially the US and EA, seem to be on an even keel, with better growth prospects than at any time since the financial crisis, or even the turn of the century, and specifically no longer dependent on rising debt ratios. The material aspirations of ordinary people are less likely to be frustrated – or dependent on unsafe increases of debt – than at any time since the 1990s.

But major risks remain, from job displacement by hi-tech, from EA imbalances, from inequality of income and wealth, from structural weakness and continued debt escalation in Japan, in diffuse fashion from effects of the emergence of China as a power equal to the US, and arguably from malignant manipulation of populist dissent by a decadent and declining Russia.

While the reach of the argument here is global, the easiest way to express the issues is by country:

USA. The prospects for aggregate real-income growth should now permit long-term gains in real household incomes, which by 2016 had merely recovered to the peak level achieved at the turn of the century in 2000. On the negative side, the displacement of jobs by tech is at least likely to continue, and could easily get worse. And the tax policies of the Trump Administration are likely to increase the inequality of income and wealth, so that serious disillusion with democracy is possible, as his appeal was based on his claim that he would improve the position of lower-middle-income Americans vis-à-vis the elite.

Meanwhile, free trade with China is threatened by resentment of its challenge to US primacy in the world, by the huge bilateral trade deficit, and by China's search for hi-tech equivalence to the US. Viewing trade as a whole, however, the US deficit has its main global counterpart in the EA surplus.

Euro area. The push for a European superstate is clearly undemocratic; the measures to achieve it, such as the replacement of the German mark by the euro, have mostly been imposed top-down, without consulting the electorate. To the extent the thrust towards a superstate is sustained, this will continue to destabilise both Europe and the world economy. German and Dutch voters have made it perfectly clear that they will not accept a fiscal union that might resolve the imbalances between (to simplify) Germany and Italy.

As long as those imbalances persist, EA policy will continue to attempt to 'export' the problem by an undervalued currency. French pursuit of a fiscal union under President Macron may achieve little more than the strengthening of anti-euro and anti-immigrant votes in Germany and Holland, and resistance from Spain.

As in the US, the medium-term economic improvement that should make populist discontent easier to handle is vulnerable to being outweighed by these other factors. Chiefly, the EA elite still hankers after making the euro system work with all its current membership, even though it was known from the outset that Italian membership would not be viable (not just through non-compliance with the misconceived 'Maastricht criteria', let alone the fallacious 'Stability and Growth Pact', later renamed the 'fiscal compact'). The 2001 admission of Greece was, of course, both a swindle and an unforced blunder. In reality, the euro system can only cease to disrupt the rest of the world, as well as underperforming itself, if it either adopts full political and economic union – ruled out by Germany and Holland – or excludes Italy and Greece, with neither solution currently 'on the table'.

Japan. Japanese populism is the dark horse in this strange race. More than the labour force of any other major country save Italy, Japanese workers have every right to be aggrieved at the poor performance of both the business elite and the other two sides of the 'iron triangle', the politicians and the bureaucracy. To stabilise the net government debt ratio at the current 130% of GDP would require inflation to rise to 4%, while despite huge efforts the Bank of Japan has not been able to get it up to its 2% target. Failing much higher inflation or a major cut in the business savings rate, the debt ratio will mount indefinitely. At some stage that may force a renegotiation of the debt – and this could be the trigger for serious discontent, since most of it is held by Japanese savers. But this is a problem that could well be a decade away.

UK. Brexit largely reflects reality, as Britain was already outside the euro and Schengen. The economic effects of Brexit seem likely to be smaller than either its advocates or opponents suppose.

The world clearly contains worse threats to future prosperity than populism. These are largely outside the reach of economic analysis. Here we see that a genuinely promising economic environment nonetheless contains within it major potential political threats from populism that has largely economic causes. The challenge for the world will be to face up to and deal with these threats, even though transnational cooperation is increasingly hard to obtain – and world government a pipe dream that would anyway probably make things worse rather than better.

Appendix 1

Time to switch tax from income to assets

The factual basis for this appendix relates to the US and UK, but the principles apply to any (and all) economy(s). It has already been argued (Chapter 11) that when it comes to taxes on individuals with higher incomes, and taxes on companies, it is inherently better to tax assets rather than income.

Income tax is an established system with long-standing means of ensuring compliance (though often not effective). But when it was conceived the rates were minimal by present-day standards. Reliance on income taxes when the rates for individuals can be as much as 50% (let alone up to 98%, as prevailed in Britain at various times from World War II till 1979) and for companies up to 35% raises entirely different issues of enforcement and fairness/equitability. It is little surprise that the compliance system has broken down.

In no country does the corporation tax (corporate income tax in America) not involve some degree of double taxation – at least as regards shareholders on high incomes, i.e. (realistically) most of them. Pension-fund shareholders may not pay any tax on dividends, but this simply introduces confusion for corporate governance. Should companies distribute dividends to suit pension-fund (and other tax-exempt) shareholders, or retain profit to relieve highly taxed individual shareholders?

The only solution that preserves intended incentives is to abolish corporate income tax. To be sure, pension-fund shareholders would then be paying no tax on dividends, but that is what was intended by making them tax-free. Company income after deduction of depreciation, and any deliberate capital allowances (e.g. for capital spending), should then be attributed to shareholders as part of their personal income, with no provision for retention to avoid tax. Foreign shareholders would be liable to withholding tax, probably at 25% (as in the US now with dividends).

Corporation tax abolition alone would almost certainly involve a loss of revenue, implicitly requiring added taxes elsewhere, and a regressive shift of income in favour of the rich. Alternative approaches to replacement of the lost revenue – notably value-added tax (VAT), but also an adapted version of the US alternative minimum tax – would retain this regressive aspect. The chief issue addressed here is the (largely unintended) redistribution of income in favour of the rich (often referred to as 'high-net-worth' individuals, HNWs). Any recognition of the almost inevitable increase of consumption taxes – which is what VAT really is – should be complemented by proposal of some means of at least preserving the current burden of tax on the rich. Ideally this rationalisation should divert people's talents from the waste of tax avoidance, a value-destroying activity.

Britain may not be such a lost cause, when it comes to tax reform, but the US appears close to ungovernable, as only tax cuts are capable of being implemented. Yet there is an unlikely source of escape from this constraint. This derives from online sales. The sales taxes imposed by a large number of US states are being eroded sharply by online sales, the use by, for example, Amazon, of people's computers in lieu of a shop. Such sales can generally be rendered tax-free by suitable sourcing. This hi-tech development means US states and localities are becoming advocates of new sources of revenue to sustain their services.

For most US states, a major form of tax revenue has always been property tax. In Britain too, local taxation has typically depended on the 'rates', or 'Council Tax', essentially a property tax.

Clearly taxes on assets are superior in economic terms to taxes on the income from assets. Suppose, for example, assets worth £100 produce an income of £5 over the average of the economy. A 30% tax on that income would yield £1.50, as would a 1½% asset tax. But compare the cases of a person generating £10 of income from a £100 asset and a person generating no income. Together they would pay the same £3 tax under either income tax or asset tax. But under the income tax, the whole £3 would come from the productive person generating a 10% return, while the unproductive person would escape any tax. Under the asset tax, however, the productive person would be paying the same £1.50 as the unproductive person, and the latter would have to reach into his/her pocket for the £1.50. If he/she was incapable of then finding a way to use the asset effectively, the asset could be sold to the productive person, raising the productivity of the economy even without he/she having to change behaviour.

It is not hard to see how this principle of the superiority of asset taxes to income taxes applies in the case of housing. With the huge baby-boomer generation entering or approaching retirement – families have already largely flown the coop – the over-occupation of housing by sheer inertia could exact a penalty that could quickly liberate supply.

The British property tax has the remarkable feature (as of now) that the property values on which the tax rate is based have not been updated since 1991. This may not involve much inequity, given its current function. The amount to be raised to finance a local authority's budget, if spread over a broadly undervalued or overvalued set of properties in a given area, will simply give rise to a higher or lower rate per pound of value. Only if major relative local price movements have occurred will the burden fall unfairly. But distortions do arise, not least between business premises and houses.

The British rates/Council Tax could (and should) be altered to permit a system of wealth or asset taxation that cannot be avoided by international shenanigans with money. Likewise, the US property taxes could (and should) readily be raised to rebalance taxation that would otherwise be relieved on the rich in the event corporation tax were largely replaced by VAT.

Realistically, US sales taxes are beyond rescue. The loss of major possible revenue to, e.g. Ireland in the case of Apple's patents lodged there precisely to avoid US taxes, would be offset if the US had a proper VAT, since that would automatically apply to all imports, including payments to Apple Ireland for the service value of using the patents. This is separate from the point that sales of products online avoid sales taxes provided they are sourced from states without a sales tax.

Will the US adopt a VAT, and solve these problems? Clearly not, in the short term. But states and localities as well as the federal government are threatened with a major loss of revenue which, if not somehow made up, will soon lead to serious erosion of public services. In a democracy, the outcome will depend on the public reaction to this. But any US VAT would have to be national (federal) rather than state or local, and its introduction as replacement for corporate income tax (whose yield is in any case now quite small) would still leave the states and localities deprived of needed revenue. If so, a resort to the only alternative, property tax increases, would healthily shift the balance in taxes on the rich towards capital rather than income.

In Britain, a revaluation of property for local tax purposes can probably not be put off all that much longer. In a country whose most scarce resource is in any case land, an object of taxation that can in no circumstances be relocated to a tax haven, increased rates/Council Tax is the natural complement of desirable abolition of corporation tax in favour of a higher VAT rate. But this could only be done after the necessary national revaluation. As local councils depend not just on their own rates/Council Tax revenue, but also on central government grants, this change could also enable a shift towards greater local independence that would be desirable in it own right.

In principle, asset taxation confined to land and buildings would be less effective than taxes on all forms of wealth. But any tax that attempted to include financial securities would be subject to similar avoidance as current income taxes. The rule of Louis XIV in France was hardly the high point of the history of governance. But his most notable minister, Colbert, did come up with the immortal observation that the art of taxation is to get the greatest number of feathers off the goose with the least hissing. By this test, wealth or asset taxation applied to financial securities is a guaranteed source of unfairness and avoidance. Land and property, on the other hand, is fixed and immoveable.

Appendix 2

Time to limit limited liability?

An awkward question exposed by the ebbing of the financial crisis is whether the 'limited liability company', a cornerstone of the world's economic system for more than a century, played a part in causing and prolonging that crisis, and therefore now needs reform.

The key word is 'reform' – abolition would make little sense. Limited liability has its roots in Victorian times, and means that a company and its owners have only limited exposure to any damaging consequences of its actions. It underpins the economies of modern capitalist societies, making possible the globalisation of capital, and much of the spread of new products and techniques of production.

But the original, nineteenth-century bargain has broken down: the state granted companies limited liability in return for paying tax and observing other obligations. Clearly this creates the chance for shareholders and senior directors to enjoy the upside from the venture, through rising share prices or big bonuses, while limiting their exposure in the event of failure or bankruptcy or extensive environmental damage. If you add to that the agility of many multinational companies in avoiding paying much tax at all, it now looks like a bad bargain.

The drawbacks of limited liability both helped cause the financial crisis, and are undermining the recovery, as well as the ability of national governments to raise the revenues they need. It is clear that reform is needed. Will incremental steps be enough, or should we try something much more radical?

Some studies of the effects of corporation tax have tended to show that it ultimately gets reflected in the price level: the after-tax return on capital in companies reverts to mean, so gross profit margins expanded over time, paying the tax. This means that its incidence, compared with straightforward VAT (sales tax), penalises successful, profitable companies in favour of the less successful. This is a perverse set of incentives. Given the additional drawbacks to be described below, perhaps it should be phased out in favour of VAT. The ultimate effects on consumer welfare should be neutral.

Modern-form limited liability originated in the nineteenth century, in the United States, as companies sought to raise capital for expansion. It is a major privilege; it allows owners (and senior directors) of the company to pursue profit through its commercial activity, while limiting their exposure to its losses or other damaging consequences of its actions – skewed incentives. Today we would say owners and directors are given a 'free option' to pursue those rewards.

In principle, in a free market, people dealing with limited liability companies are aware of this. They judge their risks accordingly, with 'eyes wide open'. But the free-market system also says there is no such thing as a free lunch. Who pays for this 'free option' given to shareholders? The answer is either randomly damaged creditors, or ordinary taxpayers, or society in general in the case of environmental damage. Experience over the past quarter-century hardly justifies idealisation of free markets. People dealing with companies do not have full information (even in theory).

The financial crisis exposed more of the serious weaknesses of limited liability – notably in the banks. Under the existing regulatory regime, liabilities of international banks had to be accepted by the state in which they happened to be headquartered – that is, by the taxpayers of that country. The collapse of Iceland's three international commercial banks in 2008 illustrated this point all too well, threatening to bankrupt a country of only 320,000 people. Had Scotland been independent in 2008, its position would have been almost as dire.

Yet these cases don't point to a problem only with banks. They hint at the flaw in the entire system of limited liability. If taxpayers are likely to be the ultimate backstop, then they should be compensated for taking this risk. They should be paid a 'premium' for the 'insurance' that they are effectively providing. This was the original deal with limited liability; in exchange for the privilege, companies would pay an extra layer of corporate tax on profits. By the 1860s, when limited liability was in place in Britain, the US and France, this deal had been explicitly codified.

Globalisation has helped erode this deal. The situation we have now unfairly benefits companies, and hurts taxpayers in the societies in which they operate, in at least three ways. The most obvious is that international firms pay less (often virtually no) tax. This means that they pay the societies in which they make their profits almost nothing for the privilege of limited liability, a privilege that largely accrues to the rich.

A second, less obvious, point is that multinational firms gain a big advantage compared to smaller, domestic companies that have far fewer opportunities to shift income out of the tax collector's reach. As smaller, domestic companies are likely to be the source of much invention – as well as providing the bulk of employment in most economies – this is obviously damaging and unfair. Globalisation has vastly increased the ability of international corporations to slip between the cracks in national laws and regulations and avoid tax. They use new technology, efficient management of a network of subsidiaries that crosses national borders and a host of financial devices to argue that they make their 'profits' only in places that have exceptionally low tax rates.

In theory, countries should be able to point to the profits earned within their borders by multinational companies, and tax them. National tax authorities are, in theory, equipped with laws that require a company to declare its national profit in a way that reflects its activity, and not to shuffle costs and income between jurisdictions using 'transfer pricing'.

In practice, however, the tax authorities' powers are often weak. The sheer complexity of the accounts and arguments about cost and pricing is one reason. Another is multinationals' potential exploitation of differences between countries in their treatment of income or capital spending. A third is political pressure on the tax authorities from governments to 'go easy' on some big companies that are bringing other benefits, such as job creation, expansion in preferred regions, support for prestige projects or any number of other government goals.

Most importantly, a company's financial managers will know far more about its affairs than any harassed tax inspector can hope to find out. Transfer pricing that reduces the tax bill can be disguised in a host of ways that are difficult to discern. A classic recent example is the location of important Apple patents in Ireland, which not only has a very low corporate tax rate, but put together a special deal on corporate tax for Apple. The company attributes huge flows of income to these patents, reducing its taxable profits in most other countries of the world.

A more abstruse example lies in how, for a long time, UK capital gains tax applied only to assets, not liabilities. In the US, a transaction that cuts the value of a debt creates taxable income. So if an inter-company transaction reduces the liability of a multinational's British subsidiary, while increasing that of a US subsidiary, a non-taxable gain occurs in Britain while a tax-deductible loss occurs in the US. This asymmetric treatment can be exploited by some highly artificial transactions.

The United States, being large, rich and the host country of the largest number of multinationals, is best placed to pressurise companies to 'own up' to what they earn within its borders – although the Apple case shows that even the US is not all-powerful. Small or poor countries are far less able to control transfer pricing by multinationals operating within their borders, given that most of the turnover will be bought in from abroad and little value added locally. They often have weak, corrupt or ineffective tax-gathering systems, and ruling elites prepared to accept pay-offs by companies.

The third source of inequity is the least visible, embedded deep in the forces shaping the world economy. It arises because the world currently has a savings glut. Why else could interest rates in major currencies stay so low, even though there is a dangerous run-up of debt compared to income (whether in the private sector or government, or both)? Some claim that this reflects monetary policies. But the relentless fall in inflation has until recently been clear evidence that monetary policy is not too slack.

Much of this book has been analysis of the damage from the savings glut, but if the world economy is to continue the current healthy recovery, it will need both more consumption (that is, less saving) and less dependence on debt. This can be achieved only if consumers have a larger share of world income, enabling them to spend more out of their income, rather than by borrowing.

How do limited liability and current corporate income taxes affect this? They motivate companies to retain too much income. When they make profits, they keep them, rather than paying dividends to shareholders or higher wages to employees. They keep hold of cash that, if it made its way to households by one route or another, would lead to more spending.

In China, Japan and South Korea, retention of large swathes of corporate income, well beyond the needs of profitable investment, seems to reflect an ingrained culture. But in the West, retention of income is mostly the result of companies building up cash in tax havens and being unable to take it out without incurring tax.

The shortcomings of limited liability have been with us for years.

The role of limited liability in worsening the financial crisis recovery is a new element. In the run-up to the crisis, it gave bankers distorted incentives to take on risk. Not that many realised they were delusional; most sincerely believed nothing could go wrong. But by giving them the reward up front, in pay and huge bonuses, well before any actual returns had materialised, limited liability contributed mightily to the carnival of folly.

For all the drawbacks of the limited liability model, is it practical to abolish it? Sadly not. A radical proposal from Professor Kotlikoff of Boston University for the reform of banking goes a long way to explaining why this is so. Kotlikoff's idea, in outline, was to turn 'banks' into mutual funds, with what are now depositors becoming shareholders in a loan-holding company. This would, he argued, ensure that losses from bad loans (and other mistaken activities) would fall on the savers that financed them, not the government. In effect, it would be banking without limited liability: loans not repaid would simply cost depositors part of their savings.

The snag in this scheme is fairly obvious. People depositing their money in a bank have no appetite for this kind of risk; they want assurance that their deposit is safe. In a more general sense, getting rid of limited liability would cause a huge contraction of commercial activity, dwarfing the problems of the world economy since 2007. Indeed, the whole network of financial markets and international financial relations depends on limited liability. There is no going back on that. Like the bank depositors referred to above, investors everywhere depend on globalised ownership patterns that have limited liability 'baked in' to their structure and behaviour.

So what could be done? The natural way forward is incremental. One suggestion has been to crack down on corporate tax avoidance, such as companies' ability to shift profits to jurisdictions with low tax rates. Tax havens are gradually lifting some of their veil of privacy.

The US is best placed to take the lead on this, but it may not go far. For instance, the US Supreme Court ruled in 2010 (in *Citizens United vs the Federal Election Commission*) that no restraint can be placed on corporate contributions to election expenses. Those are now huge and mounting fast. Many members of Congress are dependent on such funding. Luckily, US-based domestic companies resent the tax-free competition from international companies, so the populist tendency is to reduce the scope for the likes of Apple building up tax-free cash abroad. But the 'price' has been a slashing of the corporation tax rate. So far, this is simply being allowed to increase the US budget deficit (and therefore, probably, its debt). But soon this benefit to shareholders will require funding – either by cuts in social programmes or other taxes, probably mostly on less wealthy people.

There is in theory more appetite in parts of the European Union for this quest. But any serious action is highly unlikely in an organisation headed by Jean-Claude Juncker, formerly Prime Minister of Luxembourg for eighteen years. When challenged on whether Luxembourg had built its wealth out of its appeal as a regime of very low taxes, he said that companies that benefited from rulings offering very low or no taxes were taking advantage of 'the interaction between divergent national' laws, which was not the fault of Luxembourg or its administration. If those differences in tax regimes between countries were 'leading to a situation of non-taxation, then I would regret that,' he added. Given the high-level vested interests involved, the chances of any serious action in continental Europe are small.

The incremental approach is not hopeless, though any success will be limited. The foundation is much tougher enforcement of proper economic transfer pricing, working out which profits of a company have been made in each country. That task should start with national governments, led by the countries losing most at the moment. Greater international awareness of the scale of the damage, inducing more cooperation, should give courage to governments that are daunted by taking on multinational companies. The US has some clout to insist on curbing abuses in both 'respectable' havens like Switzerland and Ireland, and even outright free-rider havens such as the Cayman Islands. If it were to do so, that should enable others to follow in its wake. But the US's currently ruling Republicans are anti-tax and tend to strip the tax authorities, who take the lead in objecting to avoidance, of people and prestige.

Other incremental steps are possible. To discourage banks from taking undue risks, it would be reasonable not merely to insist that they have enough capital, but that the capital pertaining to any subsidiary's type and scale of business should be lodged in that subsidiary. In that way, the relevant profit would necessarily occur there and be taxable in the country in question – an added benefit from optimal reform of bank regulation.

Another approach might be to draw on the US concept of a minimum tax, and try to apply it to companies. This strand of the US tax code applies to people in principle liable for US tax, who would in practice otherwise largely or entirely avoid it. But such a minimum tax would almost inevitably (for companies) look a lot like a turnover or value-added tax.

That brings us to the alternative: accepting that corporation tax should be phased out because it is impossible to enforce well, and gives international companies an unfair and undesirable advantage over domestic ones. This alternative is radical, in accepting that corporation tax itself is a lost cause. (This does not exclude incremental approaches; individual countries may differ. Corporation tax is unlikely to be the vehicle by which world government is introduced!) This approach is preferable to tinkering, and is described for the US and UK in Appendix 1.

A central disadvantage is that shareholders would still not be paying anything for the immense privilege of limited liability. The skewed incentives embedded in the notion of limited liability would still be there. But the trade-off that was originally conceived has in any case been vitiated by the pass-through of the tax to consumers – and ridding the world of the other malignant effects of current corporate taxation and tax avoidance should be highly beneficial.

A radical reform on this scale could only be undertaken, however, if the regressive implications of replacing corporate income taxes with sales taxes were offset. So part of the corporate tax replacement should be some form of tax on wealth, assets or land, depending on the custom of the country. While the populist cause in the US may have for a while been hijacked by Republicans happy to pass regressive measures, this may well not prove sustainable for long.

Bibliography

Atkinson, A. B., *Inequality: What Can be Done?*, Harvard University Press, 2015

Bagehot, W., *Lombard Street: A Description of the Money Market*, 1873

Byrne, D. M., 'Does the US have a productivity slowdown or a measurement problem?', Brookings, 2016

—— 'Prices of High-Tech Products, Mismeasurement, and Pace of Innovation' (with Stephen Oliner and Daniel Sichel), American Enterprise Institute, 2017

Coase, R. H., *Essays on Economics and Economists*, University of Chicago Press, 1994

Dumas, C. E., 'US balance sheets serially trashed by Eurasian surplus', Lombard Street Research, *Monthly International Review*, No. 143, 2004

—— *The Bill from the China Shop: How Asia's Savings Glut Threatens the World Economy*, Profile Books, 2006

—— *China and America: A Time of Reckoning*, Profile Books, 2008

—— *Globalisation Fractures: How Major Nations' Interests are Now in Conflict*, Profile Books, 2010

—— *The American Phoenix: And Why China and Europe Will Struggle After the Coming Slump*, Profile Books, 2011

Friedman, M., *Capitalism and Freedom*, University of Chicago Press, 1962

—— *A Monetary History of the United States, 1867–1960* (with Anna Schwartz), Princeton University Press, 1963

Goodhart, C., 'Demographics will reverse three multi-decade global trends' (with Manoj Pradhan), Morgan Stanley Research, 2015

Kenen, P. B., *Essays in International Economics*, Princeton University Press, 1980

Keynes, J. M., *The General Theory of Employment, Interest and Money*, Macmillan, 1936

King, M. A., *The End of Alchemy: Money, Banking and the Future of the Global Economy*, W.W. Norton & Co., 2016

Lewis, M. M., *The Big Short: Inside the Doomsday Machine*, W.W. Norton & Co., 2011

Minford, P., 'What Shall We Do if the EU will not Play Ball?' (with Edgar Miller), Economists for Free Trade, 2017

Minsky, H. P., *Stabilising an Unstable Economy*, Yale University Press, 1986, McGraw-Hill, 2008

Nickell, S., 'The Impact of Immigration on Occupational Wages' (with Jumana Saleheen), Bank of England, 2015

Piketty, T., *Capital in the Twenty-First Century*, The Belknap Press of Harvard University Press, 2014

Reading, B., 'Uphill Capital Flows', Lombard Street Research, 1996

Schumpeter, J. A., *Capitalism, Socialism and Democracy*, Routledge Classics (2010), 1942

Shiller, R. J., *Irrational Exuberance* (3rd edition), Princeton University Press, 2015, (orig., 2000)

——*Phishing for Phools: The Economics of Manipulation and Deception* (with George Akerlof), Princeton University Press, 2015

Smith, A., *The Theory of Moral Sentiments*, Penguin Classics, 2010, (orig. 1759)

——*The Wealth of Nations*, Penguin Classics, 1982, (orig. 1776)

Stiglitz, J. E., *The Roaring Nineties: Seeds of Destruction*, Allen Lane, Penguin Press, 2003

UK Treasury, 'The long-term economic impact of EU membership and the alternatives', April 2016

——'The immediate economic impact of leaving the EU', May 2016

Wolf, M. H., *Why Globalization Works*, Yale University Press, 2004

——*The Shifts and the Shocks: What We've Learned – and Have Still to Learn – from the Financial Crisis*, Penguin Press, 2014

Zucman, G., *The Hidden Wealth of Nations: The Scourge of Tax Havens*, University of Chicago Press, 2015

Index